Stay True

own
Your Badass & Beautiful Life

BY LOREN LAHAV

WITH JILL MAREK +
CATHERINE KRUEGER-SULLIVAN

DEDICATION

Here's to the ones who *STAY TRUE*.The badass and beautiful women who hold fast to their values, even when the world tries to sway them.The ones who walk their own path, unapologetic, authentic—with courage in their hearts and purpose in their souls.You'll find them standing tall, straightening crowns of others while laser focused on their vision, no matter the obstacles. They see opportunity where others see fear, and they're not afraid to be bold, speak truth, shine bright, and yet humbly lead with love.They may face challenges, but they never compromise. They stay grounded, certain, present, and even more determined to live a life worth celebrating.Here's to the women who never waiver. The ones who turn trials into triumphs. Because they know that resilience isn't just about holding on—it's about growing, evolving, and whole-heartedly leading through service to make an impact.Here's to the ones who *STAY TRUE*.

CONTENTS

CONTENTS

FOREWORD

I am grateful for the endless amount of room I am given to find my own true self without question. I owe the person I am to this unconditional support from my mom.

I began applying this to every aspect of me. If there is one thing I have learned from my mom, there is no reason to tone yourself down for the sake of others' comfort.

If there is anyone who can attest to the authenticity of the woman who wrote this book it is me. My mom truly lives this every single day.

My mom has been the greatest example of staying true, from rocking her hot pink shoes on stage to sharing her personal beliefs and values to help me navigate finding mine.

She is unapologetically herself and by that, she inspires everyone around her to *stay true*.

"Stay True," is a statement that can seem so vague while to others, profound. To me, it is echoed so much in our home that it could be a mantra, yet I know it is a guiding principle.

There is always a sense of fear with showing up exactly as you are.

"These are our biggest strengths, we are *oceans of emotions*," she said. *"We are always moving and flowing but we feel things deeply and this is something that is, as I see it now, a superpower."*

Though the idea of feeling so much so intensely made me nervous for so long, it now is something I pride myself on. I wear my emotional vulnerability on my sleeve. My mom has been a role model in every aspect, but especially in navigating how to remain authentic to yourself in times when others will want you to hide.

Until I was about nine years old, I felt deeply about well - everything. So, I went to the one person I knew I always had, my mom, and she helped me understand how these feelings make us feel so deeply.

Whether your *truth* is dressing how you want or being vulnerable with your *true ideas and feelings*, if you feel judged (by others or yourself) instantly connect to your values, *stay true* to you.

With this, my style began to develop, as well as my views. There were and always will be times where *staying true* to yourself is harder to do. But, those two words come to mind immediately and it connects me back to her.

Asher Slocum

1

THE PHILOSOPHY OF "TRUE"

An authentic, and therefore, wild, Badass and Beautiful woman, living her truth is inventive, loyal, fierce and wise.

She is born both gifted and paradoxical—an intriguing riddle fueled by a heart driven to serve.

She is kind, but never tame; bold and outrageous, but enshrined with dignity. Although wild at heart, her essence is that of both ally and teacher.

She sees not just with her eyes, but with her intuition, embodying an instinctual and continued call back to nature.

She rumbles in the face of transgressions, she is fluent in the language of mysteries, and she sings songs that are both light and dark—encompassing the full spectrum and bounty of life.

No matter how many times she falls, she rises.

No matter how many times she is caged, she triumphs.

She is free; she is alive.

And in a world hungry for hope, she is what we all desperately need—because she is a force that can change the world.

—Loren Lahav, *Own Your Worth* event, Las Vegas, March 2023

I've spent the past three decades working with badass and beautiful "wild women" from all spectrums and in all stages of life, and after 36 years in the self-help industry working with alongside thought leader giants like Tony Robbins, Carolynn Myss and Wayne Dyer, I've seen firsthand the many unique trials, tests and *opportunities* that women face. With access to this extraordinary and dynamic array of world leaders, thought pioneers, and passionate truth seekers, I've continually counted myself blessed to actively bare witness and be a part of so many people's powerful stories of transformation.

Along the way, distinct patterns began to reveal themselves—showing the importance of self-awareness, resilience, and intentional action. Over time, these observations became stepping stones, shaping a practical and intuitive method that I've applied both in my own life and on stage to guide others through life's ups and downs. This method evolved into what I now call The Compass Rose, centered around four cardinal points: Inquiry, Rituals, Boundaries, and Tribe. Like a compass, these four points offer clarity in times of confusion, strength in adversity, and the courage to live a life that's authentic, vibrant, and purposeful. Which, I have affectionately called, "Own it!"

Whether you're just beginning or already well along your path, The Compass Rose, is a tool rooted in real stories, spiritual insights and personal growth, designed to help you accomplish what you are here to do. Like I say from the stage to, "Always *stay true* to who you are and OWN IT!"

It all began with my own wild and unique journey began as a lonely Jewish girl in rural North

Carolina. I went from being the person who never fit in to being the first female Army ROTC candidate from Western North Carolina. From a divorced and misunderstood single mom (that some criticized) to a mom and wife in a blended family known as an author and sought-after speaker, as a real estate investor, as a top network marketing leader for a global brand, as an entrepreneur, as a president and founder of a creative production agency, as a co-founder of a spa franchise, and now as the co-founder of a dog rescue and sanctuary. With unwavering hope for the future, I have been led time and time again back to this question and internal anchor, "Are you staying *true*?"

Let me be clear—when I say "true," I'm not suggesting the need to find or discover something new. A friend of mine once asked me, "How can you *stay true* if you don't know who you are?"

"True" is not something you need to figure out or discover; it's a divine and inherent essence deep inside you. "True" is the wild, badass and beautiful woman soul you were born with. It is the quiet voice inside that guides you, the beating of your heart when something important calls you, and sometimes, when you've strayed too far, the urgent piercing cry inside that *demands* attention. She is found in moments of uncalculated clarity, contagious laughter, crazy dance moves and overwhelming awe.

"Are you staying true?" is the question that simply brings me *back to myself.*

The problem is—the world has gotten so incredibly loud that many of us can no longer hear our own inner voice. For this reason, this book is not about *finding* yourself; it is about *owning* yourself and your truth. I believe the "wild woman" badass and beautiful archetype serves as both a reminder and a lesson; it's both a way back from and a way out of the confusion and overwhelm so many women (and men) currently face.

I'm not here to tell you who you are or to lead you on a traditional self-help journey. I'm here to lead you back to yourself and all that you *already* are. This may not be what a 43-billion-dollar personal development industry would lead you to believe, but after all my years helping others succeed, combined with my own personal trials, allow me to let you in on a little secret: You already have all the answers inside *yourself.*

The path to *Stay True* is simple, but with the chaos, noise and distractions that increasingly rob our focus, it's easy to get off track. In fact, so many women who I meet through my coaching and mastermind circles tell me they are simply "tired." And after working with them, I discover that they are in fact, not just tired, they are "exhausted." There are more energy drains in our world today than ever before. Hyper-stimulating technology and over-usage has contributed to what scientists now describe as "brain drain," a condition connected to anxiety disorder, attention deficiency and depression. Constant discord in the media and a lack of collective conversation (and therefore understanding) weighs heavily on our emotional stamina. And a system for success driven by never-ending "doing" steals valuable time from the truth and bliss of simply "being." Somehow life, with all of its conveniences, is more complicated than ever before.

At this point, finding clarity amidst the chaos has shifted from a want to a necessity. And unfortunately, there is not one simple set of instructions I can give you. We live in a beautiful, anything is possible potential—a wild web of human connection and unpredictable human complexity. Part of me wishes I could just tell you *everything* is plannable. That would make things so much easier, wouldn't it? But, also—wouldn't that be supremely boring? As long as there is life in a human, we evolve like art, a dynamic and sometimes messy process, not a destination. As we move through stages of life and key transitions, we grow in an upward spiral.

But that's also what makes my Badass and Beautiful Woman battle cry to "*Stay True*" so essential. Just as the wild, Badass and Beautiful Woman herself, our path of growth is paradoxical; it has a component that demands you step up as the creator or artist for your life. Your own inner genius contains a deep, soulful element responsible for successfully achieving your life's outcomes.

But I have one more important secret for you— I've learned over time that the only way forward is to *rise together*.

Through the years, I've always valued and relied on my pack. However, the more life I live, the stronger this reality becomes. I've learned to not just lean into others, but to proactively find ways to elevate those around me. In doing so, I've been consistently rewarded by the impact and progress we can make together.

Although a single wild, badass and beautiful woman may have the capacity to create a ripple, a pack is a tsunami force no one can ignore. Together, we have the capacity to step above the chaos, to connect and share our individual truths, and ultimately to lift each other up as high as the sky.

In this year alone, with my True Legacy Collective (TLC), I have witnessed more 'good' happen around me to better humanity in just half a year than in most entire years of my life. One of my old friends who I hadn't seen for a few years recently attended my annual *Own Your Worth* Experience in Las Vegas. Afterwards, she said to me, "Loren— the feeling of support and culture you've created to uplift others was palpable."

This is who I am and what I value most in life. At its core, this book is a call to the tribe (my pack)— to those women who want to remember the joy, beauty, strength and pride achieved from revealing the truth of their badass and beautiful selves... and to help *each other* stay there.

I've grown beyond the forest of my own personal progression and am now also asking: How do I help young women just starting their careers? How can I lend meaningful advice to others who follow my path? How can I help others navigate chapters of life that I've already experienced? How can I help those who need more joy in their lives? How can I support those who started life with less advantages than I? How can I empower others who have found themselves in a place from which it is difficult to rise? How can I help those who see me as a mentor? How can I connect people to bring even better quality of life for the greatest possible returns for all involved? How do I help my children *stay true* to themselves? And ultimately, as wild women on this journey together, *how can we help each other live, love and collectively own our worth*?

The answer I receive back, when I ask these questions, is the foundation of this book. When you attend my events and listen to my podcast, read my books, or reach out to my creative production agency—all of these life-enriching programs and resources are rooted in the philosophies and practices within these pages. This is where it all begins.

As humans, we are wired to help each other succeed; every civilization in history contains evidence of altruism. The Maasai people, one of the oldest populations living in Kenya and northern Tanzania, practice a tradition known as *"osotua,"* which translates to "umbilical cord." According to this tradition, anyone in need can request aid at any time, and in response, whoever is asked is obliged to help as long as it doesn't impact their own survival. No one keeps track of the support; no one keeps score. Although the common, modern practice of helping one another is not always as clear and beautiful as this tradition, I believe the concept is part of our genetic make-up. In fact, psychologists even have a name for this anomaly within our species; they call it "prosocial behavior."

So, let me ask you this: Are *you* living your truth? *Do you even know what that is?* Do you experience a sense of freedom in your soul? Are you awake and fully *alive*? Are you living out loud? *Are you inspiring others around you to do the same?*

This book is meant to activate *feelings* inside that will only make sense when you embody them. At one point in your life or another, these feelings will be familiar—because it's you, the real you, your truth. These are the moments (or seasons) when you were en-point, on purpose, untouchable, "on fire" and pure.

In short, it's when you were feeling so badass and beautiful, all wrapped up in one unique expression that is you and only you that you lifted up those around you as well. Any one of the tools I'm about to share in my Compass Rose Method can be the reset you need to get back on *that* path. The ability to *wake up*, stay awake, apply your own free will, make thoughtful and discerning decisions, find clarity and reignite the flame in others can only be stirred by developing your own wide, bright brush strokes. Life navigation is as unique an artform as every individual on the planet.

During this time when technology, with the rise of AI, is expanding exponentially and the world is noisier than ever, the need to be authentic, congruent and supportive of each other has never been stronger.

And in weaving the tapestry of my life so far, I've created, re-created, and refined techniques that continually help myself and others either "*stay true* to you" or "return to self." The wisdom I've collected along the way is valuable. For me, the urge to stir the women of the world wide awake is profound. I don't want the as Wayne Dyer called it "music to die within" me (or you!), and *I'm done playing small*. This book is my opus—a wide beacon and rally call to women from every age and stage as well as every walk of life.

These are tools that work. They've been through it all—the fire, the earthquake, the tornado... and everything in between. Eventually, I've found there is a balance in all the paradoxes life has to offer—being certain and happy while simultaneously wanting to share more, be more, expand more and learn more.

I want all of this for you. I want you to *remember* the joy, beauty, strength and pride that stems from living your unwavering personal truth. Let this book be first your wake-up call to *Stay True*, then a roadmap you can open and unfold as needed, continually expanding and growing in your own wild, badass and beautiful, and weaving ride forever onward.

2

THE BADASS AND BEAUTIFUL RIDE

Life is fluid, evolving, and barely predictable—sort of like a stream. In this way, it is just as easy to get caught in the flow as it is to get carried away and lose focus when the rocky parts impede progress. Navigating a "true" course in life isn't a pre-marked trail complete with caution signs and "time to your destination" courtesies. Instead, it's more like a finding your place in one of those old-school theme park wave pools. It's smooth, peaceful and simple... and then all of a sudden (as if someone flipped on the crazy wave switch), *it's not*. The journey is sometimes about moving through the chaos, sometimes about forward momentum, and sometimes just about holding on for dear life. How does one plot a course through something so wild? It's not linear.

I have a hunch that at some point in life (perhaps right now) you've drifted away from your true self. It's likely that at least once you have "hidden" your personal genius to make a situation better for someone else—only to hurt yourself in the end.

How do I know this? No matter what chapter of evolution you're in right now, odds are good that you've probably been through some stuff. We all have.

Why is it when we hit the dark, rocky shores of the challenging phases of our lives, we finally take the time to get real with ourselves? Meanwhile when life hums along in stale but steadfast beats, it's so easy to get caught up in the noise and "get carried away" from who we really are? Away from our own *true self*? By consistently sabotaging our own happiness to simply "fit in," to "just get things done," or "just make everyone happy," we forget our power to break our own unsupportive patterns.

Twenty-seven years ago, I wrote my first book, *No Greater Love*, which was a guide centered around my first child, Josua and what was then my new role as mother. The book gained attention early on, and many people told me it gave them real and useable insights that reinforced both the blessings and adventures of parenting.

I worked hard to promote the book initially, but after the book had been out for a few years, I was offered a position to launch, re-design, and facilitate a flagship program, Life Mastery, for Tony Robbins at his resort in Fiji. My kids' father and I moved our young family—Josua, as well as our second-born, Quinn, around the world and into the jungle. We were busy there—teaching, organizing and producing a new event every week for two-and-a-half years straight (36-week-long-programs a year).

Let's just take a moment to talk about what I just said. Launching a new program deep in the center of Fiji was both an exhilarating and daunting experience. The sheer beauty of the lush, untamed landscape was a stark contrast to the emotional and physical toll it took to make the vision a reality. Far from the comforts of modern life, the challenges quickly mounted—unpredictable weather and conditions in the perfect blend of limited resources. Every day brought a new test of resilience and resourcefulness. Navigating cultural differences, weather, and logistical setbacks—ensuring the program's success. Yet, through the sweat, exhaustion, and occasional doubt, the journey became a testament to our will, pushing boundaries spiritually, physically, and mentally. It was my time on a rock in the Pacific and I wouldn't trade it for the world because it has made all of the difference.

Let's just talk resources. Just imagine, everything you take for granted now did not even exist. We are talking wired phones and dial up internet. Cell phones were not what they are now. They were phones. For the most part, we still used phones with wires that connected to the walls, not small computers in your hand. There was no FaceTime. There was no Zoom.

Living on an island made these technological delays even worse. We had to wait for most of the files we needed to be sent in big boxes filled with cases of VHS tapes and silver CDs that had been uploaded with the information we needed to run these events. Jump drives were not a thing.

With so much going on, in many ways, I lost track of the book.

Out of the blue, my good friend, Heidi, a branding and public relations powerhouse, widely regarded as one of the best in the industry, called me one day. This was not your average Zoom call of today. Back then, a phone call to Fiji from the Mainland of the US was sometimes as clear as mud. You could barely hear the person on the other side. The line would actually crackle with this electric sound and at times the voices would cut out intermittedly. It was more like a game of wordle than a conversation—trying to figure out what the person on the other side was saying.

Heidi has always been one of my biggest fans. She supports all of my ideas and has attended every event she could physically get to. She was so excited on the other side of that crackling phone line.

"Don't screw this up," she said as I picked up the phone.

"You're about to get a call from the most popular day-time television show in the United States. They want you to come on the show. Don't screw it up, ok?"

A short time later, the phone rang.

Sure enough, it was the Studio. The produceer shared with me that my book was the talk of the office. They had passed it around and the team was in love.

My heart raced; my palms were drenched. I'm pretty sure I had to remove a layer of clothing, I was sweating so hard with anticipation. This was a lifelong dream! My thoughts repeating, "I am going to be on THIS SHOW!!! These people want me on THEIR SHOW!!!! Here it comes..."

"We want you to do a show," she said.

"Sure," I said, "What's the topic?"

She shared, "The topic is—how to get your husband to do more around the house."

A vibration went through me like the wrong note hit on a piano (And trust me I have played a wrong note or chord in my life here or there). Everything in my body knew this was off-key for me. I took a big deep breath, sighed, and thought to myself, "Oh, I am so going to screw this up."

After a long pause I said, "I'm not your girl."

Another long pause.

"I actually don't want to be known as the girl who got her husband, and all of the other husbands in America, to do more around the house. My husband (at the time) and I do not have that kind of relationship. This is not who I am. If you're asking me how to be more resourceful, I could spend some quality time on that topic. But how to trick my husband into doing more – that's not me."

The call ended pretty well. I was honored she thought of me. In the end, I didn't feel like I had screwed up. So many times, we have expectations of how it is working – versus how cool it is to even get that chance.

My friend called me a short time later upset, "You've just turned down the world's most popular studio," she said.

"Yeah, I know. But I don't want to be known as 'that girl,'" I said.

When other people ask you to get involved with a surface-level "dream project," it is easy to "fall for everything" in the path to achieving. Getting caught up in the excitement of more money, more visibility is intoxicating, however, it can also drain your soul. If you spread yourself thin trying to make everyone happy, the one person who will suffer is you.

This is why I do what I do – to help people understand that some things just take time. Life isn't only about embracing the sweet-smelling roses. Nor is it about quick-fix highs. For that matter, living so "safely" that the process becomes numb and sterile, is also not badass nor beautiful.

This is an example of what I think of as that due North point of your Compass. When you are true to yourself you set yourself free from the opinions and expectations of others. Checking in with yourself and asking, "*Am I being true to me*?" This keeps you solidly on your path. Which is essential to achieving your outcomes and aspirations. Without this direction from staying true, you lose sight of the goal and it is easy to become overwhelmed.

A few years passed, and my family relocated back to the United States.

I received a second book-related call. This time, the Ronald McDonald House in Portland, Oregon, was on the other end of the call, "We love your book, and we want to give it to all of our 175 patients' mothers on Mother's Day."

"Awesome," I said as I hung up the phone and began to scramble to figure out where and how to find 175 copies of my book. This was in the days before on-demand printing and my book was no longer "in print."

It didn't take long before I figured out that the only way to fulfill the Ronald McDonald House's Mother's Day request was to run a complete reprint—which included new, updated photography and re-editing. My friends told me I was crazy. The wholesale profit of 175 new books was much less than what it would cost me to re-print the book.

Even with the scope and scale of the project so far out of balance, there was something telling me I needed to do it.

And so, I did. I listened to my heart.

Literally just a week after I made this decision, I got a third call about the book. This time from a buying agent. "I just got your book into Target. They're asking for 30,000 copies. Can you have them ready in two weeks?"

I nearly fell off my seat.

The book was already in production. However, to get that many copies so soon, I had a couple of complicated hoops (and risks) to mitigate. How many of you have been there before? What you know is the right thing to do looks like an uphill battle to everyone around you—and yet beyond all explanation, it is a MUST.

First of all, I had to personally visit the printer to streamline the process and approve the proofs in time. Second, the cost to produce 30,000 books was over six digits–out of my pocket (which I did not have). This was a huge opportunity and this one was a real pull. I figured it out.

And, even after Target purchased the finished books from me, if they were damaged or didn't sell, I would be responsible for buying them back.

The first issue—getting to the printer in China— miraculously fixed itself. A few days after receiving the Target call, I was asked to work another event—in China. What's more? It turned out that my printer was less than two miles away from the event venue. (That event was literally me, the AV guy, and a security guy. Talk about a G-d moment or a universe nudge.)

With that affirmation and momentum behind me, I rolled the dice and my mom said, "Let's do it!" My Dad had just passed away and she said,

"This is what your Dad would want me to do." She loaned me the publishing fee. Fortunately, amazingly, and over time, most of the books sold. I was able to donate some of the profits to moms in need and I was able to pay my mom back. However, the best part of this story was still in the making.

"Trade your expectations for appreciation and the world changes instantly," a big thing I learned from Tony Robbins. Because I was still putting finishing touches on our new home in Las Vegas, I was spending an irregularly frequent amount of time (and money) visiting our local furnishings store. I could be found there on a semi-regular basis. Let's just say, I was there enough that the employees began to recognize me. One of the customer service reps I started to get to know, was an opinionated and consistently unhappy, tattooed man. He often helped me load my car with heavy furniture and accessories.

Eventually, we developed a bit of a friendship. Enough so that one day, I asked him about his tattoos. I'd noticed them all from the beginning, but I'd been curious about one in particular on his inner forearm—it was a quote from my book.

"I don't want to talk about it," he dismissed me.

"I'm going to find out," I thought to myself. Then, I asked if he would help me carry my things to the car.

As we were walking, he said, "you see I don't make a lot of money here..."

He stopped and looked me in the eyes as he kept both hands on my cart filled with household goods. The words that followed were raw, "See, I don't make a lot of money here, but everything I make, I send to my family out of the country. I've been looking for another job and was offered the opportunity to sell oxycontin on the street. I knew I could make a lot of money doing that... but it's not *who I am*."

"So, I was sitting in the breakroom eating my sandwich one day, thinking about how I was going to kill myself to just end it all. I look over, and there's this 'mommy' book on the table that belonged to a girl who just had a baby. For some reason, I picked it up and flipped it open. The page it landed on had this quote," he said pointing to his wrist.

"Those words really struck me," he said. "It gave me hope that there is something more for me, and so... I decided not to kill myself."

We began loading my car with packages. I reached beyond my daughter's car seat and into a cardboard box on the floorboard of the car. As he turned to close the door behind the last of my shopping, I handed him a fresh copy of my book.

"Wait. Why do you have this?" he asked.

"Hello! Look a little closer," I said, pointing at the cover.

His eyes got really wide as he looked from the cover of the book to my face. All at once, he got it. "Your book saved my life," he told me.

In that moment, all the steps of raw and unrelenting *truth* that I had taken made complete sense. It was all worth it.

You are probably wondering what the quote was? The quote was "To be a person you are not; is to waste the person you are."

I didn't make it onto that famous tv show. I didn't take the instant hit or the fast-track success route. I wasn't ready. I really wasn't. I wanted it, but the timing wasn't right. I still had things to learn. I still had to evolve. Timing is everything. Sometimes, you have to be patiently persistent. Sometimes, you need to realize you just need to go deeper. This is the story unfolding.

On this badass and beautiful life journey, you have to be strong enough to let go if it isn't true to you and patient enough to wait until it is.

Recently, after my True Voice event for TLC in Utah...I had a participant come up and tell me after, "I was missing the richness. I was so in my head. If I allowed myself to feel vulnerable and say, "I never thought I'd fit in. I would have been able to relax and be more present."

I couldn't tell her why it had to happen this way— all I know is that it wasn't her time yet at the event. She needed to feel what she felt (agony, angst, pressure) to fully embrace her truth on the other side.

In the past, if you asked me why I didn't do it, I would have said, "... because it wasn't *me*." Now, I am able to say "I chose to *stay true* to myself, and that decision resulted in something far greater." A man's life was saved, and as a result, his family did not have to experience the trag- edy of his loss. All because I chose to honor my truth.

A few years ago, friends of mine asked, "That studio loved your personality and your book. Why did you say no?"

I explained, "If I had taken them up on their offer back then, it would have been false. My message is to *stay true to yourself*." If I would have fit my message into the constraints of the show's topic, I would have been doing the exact opposite of what I want people to get."

The beauty of this winding road is that I can still hold my head up high. It would have been easy to just say yes. But, the glory on this path to a *badass and beautiful* life is found in the long game.

To that end, life is about "embracing the suck," as much as the success. To take it a step further—I'm *grateful* for the suck. If I hadn't gone into the trenches, embraced my fears and fought for my truth, I wouldn't be who (or where) I am today. I love who I have become. I have finally become the badass and beautiful woman I wanted to be. Heck ya!

The trenches are where the work begins so the real you can shine. This is where my Compass Rose Method comes into play. **You Inquire** (your True North), asking questions of yourself to gain clarity on who you are. By maintaining **Boundaries** around who you know you are and where you are going. You step back to integrate the **Rituals** that you know will bring you back into balance as you manifest your magnificent badass and beautiful life, and you surround yourself with a **Community** (tribe/pack) who supports you. If these four points do not align, its a "no go." No matter how attractive the offer.

The sexy stuff on the surface may give you certainty and a sense of safety. However, when you start to wonder why you're not succeeding (or more importantly not feeling fulfilled)— it's because you're not celebrating who you are behind the scenes. There's something intangible and remarkably wild about building a life that is pure and real; it is the essence and the energy of *Staying True*.

It's easy to look at someone else's success and not understand or observe all of the steps it took to get there. But what's behind the scenes is the *good stuff*. That's what makes or breaks *true* success (on the inside) and where all the fun happens.

Twenty-three years ago, when I was first working in Fiji for Tony Robbins, leading his Life Mastery events, I had a similar breakthrough. After I first got the opportunity, I spent my first few events literally trying to be the female version of Tony (whatever that is). I'd try on certain facial expressions, throw out my power moves and make larger-than-life gestures to capture the audience. Eventually, I found myself asking, "Why is this not working?"

The answer came back loud and clear...If I wanted to make an impact, which I did, I had to focus on being the best *me*, not Tony. I realized that I didn't have to be six foot seven to change the world, or to make an impact, but I did have to *Stay True* to me.

This can be a point of confusion. We put ourselves (and others) into boxes. We create expectations. We work to live up to them—both perceived and real. We strive to make *other* people happy. We create checklists of supposed successes. We put our best *face* forward because we *think* it's what the world wants. But is it?

I am a reflection of a person who has done the work. I have taken what I learned and applied it. Because of this I am truer to myself.

That said, I learned so much from Tony Robbins. He is true to himself. He was criticized for a long time for being a self-proclaimed, "Artist forming souls." He turned off the noise. He just kept doing it. He didn't buy into the thought that he wasn't enough. That he wasn't worthy. He owned his worth. He is true. Every year I am more and more inspired by him. Just last night he raised $2 million from 1400 people to help kids who are human trafficked. He is the real deal. He lives to do all he can to make the world better each day.

One more example. When I was 15 years old I was comparing myself to others. I always struggled with my confidence. I was short, didn't have a boyfriend, and had big boobs for my size. I felt like everyone was telling me what was wrong with me. I was listening to the noise. I was out of touch with all of the beauty that was inside me. Rumi has a quote, "Look inside yourself everything you want you already are..."

Leading up to that moment, I didn't have gratitude for me. I was seeking acceptance from others. Looking for compliments and reinforcement from the outside.

My Mother's prompt (and surprising) reply to me was, "I guess I haven't done my job."

I was taken back.

I said, "Mom, what do you mean? You've done a great job."

She replied, "If you need someone to tell you that you are beautiful, then I haven't done my job."

The key message that I took away from this conversation with my mom in the 1980s was this: *Somebody else is not going to hand me fulfillment. My joy, my sense of achievement will come from what I cultivate on the inside. I am responsible for my own happiness.*

Are you with me? Am I making sense?

The short-cut to your happiness lives inside of you and only you and I am here to help you OWN IT through these four: Inquiry, Rituals, Boundaries, and Tribe. There are chapters dedicated to each of these four; however, just as an actual compass goes around in circles and swings back and forth—you will find a combination of these throughout the pages of this book.

For instance, a Ritual that began around age 15 years old, as a result of my Mom's advice, was to pull out the picture of myself at age 5-years-old. I started then and to this day still keep a framed picture of myself on my desk. I look to "her" for inspiration. What would she think of this moment? Would she proud of me? What advice would she have for me? Now and then I look at her and let her know, "This is part of us becoming who we are."

Another ritual that came to me about this time is the one of looking myself in the mirror and having gratitude for who I am.

There is a way to break the cycle.

Each of us are in the real-world living—doing dishes, doing the laundry and picking up after our dogs. Toiling away, jumping through hoops, checking off the to-dos, solving problems, paying bills, worrying about all the many unknowns, sleeping, waking up, and doing it all over (and over) again—it's easy to end up feeling like you are sitting at the bus-stop passively watching the world cruise by.

The thing is—many people fall asleep at the wheel of life. Caught up in the mundane, it's easy to forget our own *power*. This is huge; it's the key ingredient.

I was supposed to go to Liverpool to speak and I was going back and forth because the shooting had just happened in Las Vegas. I didn't want to leave the country. My friend, Heidi, knew how much

I admired and respected Oprah. Heidi got a lot of her clients and Tony on the Oprah platforms for her talk show and later even on her network OWN.

When she was invited to the Wisdom of Sunday book party in Santa Barbara, Heidi plotted with Z to surprise me. They told me I was going to visit a church, "*Put on your Sunday best!*"

As we entered the long driveway leading to the valet, I realized this wasn't a church. Well actually, it ended up being one of the most soulful, special moments.

It was the promised land. Yes, the home of my vision board regular. The lady who raised me and so many others by showing up in living rooms around the country daily via television where she was a shining example of living her truth. This was a dream come ***true***.

As we get out of the car, the first person I see is Brendan Burchard. I've known Brendan Burchard for a long time. He greeted me saying, "Wonderful to see you here."

Someone else I've known for a long time as well says the same thing. A part of me didn't get it. I had put all these people on a pedestal for so long.

It was a beautiful afternoon. At the end of the day, I had yet to meet the host, "I should be grateful I'm at Oprah's house. Come on Loren, just be grateful you are here. Show some gratitude."

Heidi called, "Come on Loren it's time."

I was surprised again, "Time for what?"

"Your time to meet Oprah," Heidi returned.

I thought to myself, "It's been a long day. I'm sure the last thing she wants is to meet another person."

Life unfolds in a beautiful way. What did I say to Oprah?

"You know, most people fall asleep at the wheel of life. I think our job is to *wake people up* and keep them *awake*."

Oprah nodded in agreement.

"Thank you for what you said," she replied as she hugged me.

I was waiting for permission to really own my worth. Even though others gave me permission (such as Brendan Burchard in the valet), I still didn't give myself permission. I still didn't have the courage to say, "You've got this!"

I was doing great and good things for others. I was connecting with a large percentage of the whole world – and still I didn't give myself space to OWN IT.

One of my TLC girls, Margaret, put it well when she said recently on a call, "I had a breakthrough– I've written the books, I've created the programs, I have the companies, and the non-profit organization, but I realized I was cheating myself by not playing bigger."

 What I've done is more than 99.9% of people in the world – but why is this an excuse? There is always another level. Why am I not going to the next level?

Just three years ago when I did my first Own Your Worth event. I had to take big ass risks. I was scared s@4*less. I knew I had to do it. It became my must. Equal parts exhilarating and terrifying.

How many of you know that undeniable thrill that comes with stepping into the unknown? Heart racing, mind churning with "what ifs." Feeling both empowered and vulnerable at the same time. Doubts crept in and I kept going. I took the leap of faith, where logic and instinct collided. As a result of my Own Your Worth event, life has completely and magnificently transformed (not just for me, but for every woman who attended— no exaggeration).

And so, to you, my friend, reading these words— this is *your* formal invitation your permission slip. This is the sign. The feather's touch. Whatever it takes to wake up—and to stay awake for the rest of your life.

Now that *you* are here on this journey with me, take your car off cruise control. Cruise control is boring. Cruise control is stuck. Cruise control limits yourself. It allows you to take your foot off the accelerator.

How's that working for you? Maybe it's time to put your foot down and activate. You set your speed.

Is your speed so comfortable your future self will have regrets? Is this why you picked up this book?

I compel you to embrace it all. This is *your* journey, *your* truth, *your* wild woman, badass and beautiful, choose-your-own-adventure. Get ready to move forward from here with thoughtful (true) purpose.

I don't know about you – but I'm so excited for you. Let's do this! It's time to OWN YOUR WORTH!

STEP 1:
TRUE VOICE

3

SET YOUR COMPASS

An authentic woman, living her divine truth is paradoxical—badass and beautiful. Women encompass the full spectrum of beauty through birth, pain, love, and loss—life.

I've learned that while we as women share many commonalities in our life journeys, we are also incredibly multi-faceted, each with a message as unique as the individual. This is why I have a diamond at the front of every manual I produce.

Created through pressure despite and inclusive of the environment where they are discovered, diamonds are like women. Timeless, precious, rare, and enduring. Reflecting light in all directions just as each woman has within her leader, warrior, creator, nurturer—every role emerging with unmatched brilliance. Vibrant and diverse, each woman's wisdom and authenticity, are like a diamond's clarity. Freedom achieved from expressing, is her radiance.

This is how the True Voice Intensive came to be. There's a clear progression to fully owning your worth. To truly embrace it, a woman must first share her story, what I call, "*truth*" from a safe and sacred space. The Hawaiians call this "Talk Story."

There is a profound metamorphosis as women engage in the True Voice process. I watch as the protective shells fall away, revealing their true essence. In this transformation, a powerful shift occurs. The fire that emerges from deep within mirrors their inner strength, enduring and learning while overcoming their soul's greatest challenge. It's a process of rediscovery, where they embrace what was always within. And it all starts with Inquiry.

The result is nothing short of an ignition—a spark that sets in motion a powerful propulsion into the life they've always envisioned. It's as if the barriers that once held them back are suddenly lifted, allowing them to move forward with unstoppable momentum. This newfound confidence creates a surge of energy, converting aspirations into actions that bring un-matched purpose and determination. They no longer simply dream of the life they desire; they actively create it, fully embracing the limitless possibilities. Stepping into the fullness of their life.

In awe, I watch. Noticing the gift of *every* woman is *desperately needed* right now. Especially as the world gets seemingly more extreme, these guiding principles are vital to human evolution.

What was your first life defining moment? The moment in time when you put both feet on the ground and stood up for your "truth?"

For me, it all began when I was walking down the hall in grade school and heard a boy shout, "The Jews deserved to die in the Concentration Camps..."

The shouting kids all around me froze my senses – it was deafening. A pint-sized fifth grader, I maneuvered around the other kids. Pushing through the electrified, crowded hall and into the middle of the pack. There, I found a schoolmate pinned by two other boys as a red-faced bully yelled, spit flying, his forehead practically touching the face of the other as he screamed about blacks and Jews.

In one movement, I put my 10-year-old foot down and shouted, "No more!"

I leveraged my school-bus-shaped lunch box between the two boys and pushed the lead-bully off of my schoolmate and into a locker.

A quiver of core truth rippling in my spine, I felt raw in every part of my body. With resolute, I knew that from here forward, I would no longer tolerate bullying. There would be no more playing small. I would stand up for what matters. From here forward, I would forever *stay true* to myself.

Ultimately, I felt relief. To finally break free of the fear and to stop yielding to my desire to "fit in." In this new skin, I realized that staying true is a *feeling*—one that can only be understood when embodied completely.

On stage, I often give the example of a snake shedding its skin. Snakes' skin does not grow with its body. At one point, a snake can no longer grow unless it first sheds the old layer of skin. Sometimes the old layer has parasites that could harm the snake. Humans seem to do this with old beliefs. We have to shed old patterns of thought in order to grow. Just like the snake, you are going to have to let go of the old layer so you can continue to grow.

To *stay true* is to be authentic and genuine, in a noble "even-if-no-one-likes-me" sort of way.

That day in the school hallway with the bullies, something deep inside me had been hidden. Now, released and acknowledged, I felt *strong* and somehow clean within myself.

Have you ever felt like this? Have you ever felt life rush out like a tidal wave, holding nothing back? Everything—fear, sadness, joy, or relief—all at once. And even if it gushed out messy and unfiltered, how did it make you *feel*? Did it make you feel alive? Were you relieved? Did you feel like, "FINALLY!" Did you feel exhilarated? There's a moment of intense vulnerability followed by a sense of freedom, unraveling, and deep release.

This is what it feels like to *stay true*. What do you need to be reminded of in order to *stay true*?

Let's go deeper.

I was raised, in Asheville, NC in the 1960s and 1970s. In some ways, it was a different world. Yet, as much as the world changes, it stays the same. Back then, nobody knew where Asheville was, I'd have to explain "between the Smokey and Blue Ridge Mountain ranges."

It's funny, now Asheville is a destination. Back then, the Biltmore Estates was the attraction. We always had to go somewhere else to get whatever it was others, from more metropolitan areas, took for granted. For instance, we had to drive to Atlanta for something as simple as call it "Ash-Vegas" because there was literally nothing to do.

Now, people plan their whole lives to visit; but, for my brother and me, two Jewish kids in Catholic school, life was limited. You are probably wondering why the heck did you go to a Catholic school? It was my parents' way of teaching us resilience.

Their belief was that life would be hard. "People aren't going to always be agreeable. You have to learn to thrive outside of popular opinion," they would tell us.

I know this is hard to believe, but at that time, in this region, a few of the neighborhoods still had by-laws against allowing "Jews and blacks." My parents told us, "Not to make a fuss." We were told to, "Just keep quiet." But truth was, it hurt.

My parents had the best intentions. They believed they were giving us the highest quality life in the country with the best education available. However, my brother likes to say the greatest lesson we learned between 1971-1978 was how to effectively stop a nosebleed.

We were not "high society." People thought of us as "nice people." We were known to be very "middle class." Hard working. We never went on a family vacation because my Dad was always working.

My father was an optometrist and had his own practice. He cared deeply about everybody and was up early every day making sure his patients were taken care of. He participated in every non-for-profit and philanthropic cause. My mother had a shop in town and would try anything. Today, we would call her style, "ahead of its time."

For the most part, my brother and I kept to ourselves socially. I remember wondering "why" there seemed to be a lack of party invitations in our mailbox. Was it something I said? Was it me? Was it my brother? Our parents? Was it because we are Jewish?

It's crazy what we start to make up in our heads. One of the key elements of this book is Inquiry (asking questions to bring you back to True North). Think of the pain I could have saved myself if I had the courage to ask for the truth.

How many times have you created an emotional hot mess of an internal drama for yourself as a result of a story you made up in your head without first Inquiring? When people fall into a downward spiral of seeking validation on the outside and feeling denied (truth or not), brains begin to form definitions and theories that may or may not be true to support your thoughts.

That said, my first love was in the shadow of religion. His parents forbade us to date because he was Catholic and I was "the Jewish girl."

I can remember standing on the manor grounds near his blue mustang convertible. We had had such a great day, "I love being with you, we have so much fun; but, I can't date you anymore because you are Jewish," he told me.

None of this made sense. I didn't understand why I wasn't accepted. All I had ever wanted was for people to love me for who I am. Why did the details of my heritage and religion matter?

I'm not sharing this with you for a pity party. I'm letting you know this was a pain I had to overcome as a kid. I'm not alone. We all have a social challenge to overcome in youth. It seems now more than ever.

I wasn't happy because I felt different. It sucked at the time. I didn't understand. I didn't want to be resilient. I wanted to feel light and included. Now, I realize what a gift it was.

Some people might be reading the book saying, "What Loren!? I loved you!"

Now, as a mother I support my daughter as she navigates the muck between antisemitism and other sub-cultures considered alternative. This is life.

Asher compares her teenage years as a Jew in the 2020s to the Shinagawa Monkey in, "Confessions of the Shinagawa Monkey." Disconnected from both sides. The Shinagawa Monkey was raised with humans and then no longer fit in either community (human or monkey) once his professor friend passes away. She says, "I never fully felt a part of my Jewish Community because I am not a traditionalist and I have never fully felt a part of my subculture because they don't understand why I am Jewish."

That is just what I felt a generation earlier. I was different and I didn't understand why it was such a big deal.

When I realized religion was at the root of some of this monkey business, I became religion-curious. I studied as many forms of religion as I could. I was excited about learning and was able to appreciate all kinds of people. I took my Dad along to "try them all."

I wanted to see what religion was all about. I attended services from Billy Graham Revivals to Robert Schuller and the Crystal Cathedral. I went to the Pentecostal Church. It was fun. I tried them all. I wanted to appreciate vs judge other people's faiths. That became my mission. I am grateful that these challenges came to me because I wouldn't have gotten so curious otherwise. Don't discount those things that have made you stronger.

At my events we work through the pain of our stories until we are able to have the lessons that are meant for us come through us. Talk about polishing the diamond! We recognize people who tell stories with: The Courage, The Wisdom, The Magic, and The Heart Awards. The person who incorporates all of these pieces is nominated by the entire audience to win The Ruby Slipper Award. These people have, like Dorothy and Toto, successfully come full-circle in their own healing process.

Recently, something remarkable happened Michele, our Ruby Slipper Award recipient, had healed so thoroughly from telling her story the night before that she could no longer remember the details the next day.

Hearts swelled with happiness for Michele because we realized as a collective that "she had a new story." She learned what she needed to know and was ready to move on. This is what life is about. Allowing the pain part of your memories to fall through the sieve until all that remains is the lesson "gem" worth keeping.

What made all the difference for Michele was the sisterhood in the room kindly holding space for her to process these lessons.

Asher, who helps me run my events, gives this take-a-way, "You have to build your own community. You can't wait to be accepted into somebody else's circle. Find people who value you for who are without having to cut off parts of yourself for acceptance."

Like we did for Michele, find people who make you feel "wanted" who support while you do the work to own your voice.

This realization has allowed me to create a space where I can be open and authentic, talking about everything from antisemitism to implicit biases that shape our perspectives without us even realizing it. We must acknowledge these biases, engage in meaningful conversations, and stay open to shifting our perspectives. This is Owning TRUTH.

I learned that acceptance isn't always guaranteed. Instead of waiting for others to accept me, I chose to embrace my voice, selectively build my circle, and constantly work on creating an inclusive space for myself and others. These experiences have shaped who I am today, teaching me the importance of owning my Identity and fostering genuine connections like those in my events, TLC and Manifest Memberships.

My conviction to *stay true* to myself was seriously tested in those early years. Layer by layer, I've healed and begun to release the shell of protection around my truth.

Among these other more difficult themes of self-acceptance and rising above the fray, I consider my childhood to be an education in the art fo the flea market. I like to say I grew up there.

Every Saturday and Sunday, at 4 am, as a family of four, we would unpack hundreds of banana boxes filled with treasures to sell for a quarter each out of the back of our family car. Dreamland Drive-in Flea Market wasn't a trendy, chic open-air market of today, but rather a place where the fleas had fleas. All-day unwrapping tchotchkes from newspaper we schlepped from our garage, what my Dad called, "The Appendage on the side of our house." He would follow the comment with, "You know people typically park cars in that."

Old salt and pepper shakers, old Pillsbury Doughboy signs, a 6-foot glow-in-the-dark Elise the Borden Cow, Arts and Crafts Devil jugs, old Dutch boy and girl miniatures, old... being the common theme. There we were, setting up "shop" in the name of "building character and fostering" for my brother and me.

My parents wanted us to build real-world skills. They believed that when my brother and I made sales and collected money for our services, it was a great way to get positive feedback from other adults outside the family. They saw starting our own leather goods business as a way to boost our confidence, and figuring out how to sell was a lesson in work ethic. And honestly, they were right. The experiences they gave us built the muscle we have used to thrive as adults in the world beyond Asheville. Our work ethic and ability to effectively communicate in diverse circumstances are some of our greatest gifts.

Hundreds of unique every day, hard-working people from all over the region came to our station wagon with the drop-down table in back. My brother and I had a card table with squeaky legs we used to set up our booth next to the station wagon. We made leather key chains, belts, and bracelets with stamped and painted lettering to sell.

It was hard work. We were bone-tired and sunburned at the end of the day. The whole family would collapse into bed after counting our coins. There was no Zelle. We weren't even collecting bills. We brought home a can with coins at the end of our long days in the sun. We had so much appreciation for every little thing because we understood what it took to earn something coin by coin.

The stories, people, and experiences I encountered each of those weekends will forever be a part of my personality's DNA.

I know this is why I am always on the search to find the perfect "something special" gift for people in my life. In fact, I am known for making the best-ever "swag bags" for my event participants. During those long-hard days at the flea market I began to notice patterns in people. And in turn, learned what lights people up.

There's something universal about seeing that spark or child-like joy when something feels "just right" for someone. Whether it's fulfilling a want or a need, these moments serve as anchors, reminding the recipient that we are connected on this journey and that their uniqueness has been truly seen and appreciated by me. Whether it's a silver bracelet engraved with "*Stay True*" or a leather vest that inspires them to embrace being "Badass and Beautiful," these gifts are expressions of love and gratitude for the time we've shared.

After my years at the flea market, I keep the furnishings in my house to a few, simple reminders of people, experiences, and sentiments. On my desk, I keep three objects:

Compass: to stay on track
Goggles: to stay focused
Crown: to remind me that I am a queen

Have you ever held a compass? A magnetic compass works because the Earth itself is a gigantic magnet... and so are we.

Did you know there are actually three moving parts to align before you are able to receive the directional reading? First, there is a tiny pendulum that must be aligned with a tiny hole (like an old-fashioned children's ball and cup game). Next, there is a sundial element. Finally, the actual direction.

That tiny hole is so frustrating. Who remembers trying to play that game? Just when you think, "I'm never going to get it – it's never going to happen..." it falls into place.

Ultimately, it takes patience. Gently engage your heart and mind, breathe, relax – finally it goes. The tiny shifts are what make the difference. What in life is like that for you?

Then, the Sundial. Internally the conversation might go like this, "I don't know how to read this thing! I'm not smart enough!" How many ideas die because you believe you don't have the skill? Sometimes what seems steeped in mystery is much simpler than it at first seemed. Like a new interface when your phone updates, "Don't let it beat you!" Take it one step at a time. These days hacks are everywhere. The secret is taking it one step at a time. Find what you need to learn and then schedule the time to into your day.

Can you imagine traveling this globe's vast oceans with nothing but this small, brass tool to guide you safely to shore? Especially with so many moving parts?! And honestly, we know it didn't always work out according to plan—que the Pilgrims landing on Plymouth Rock (they were at least a thousand miles North of where they intended); but, for the most part, once these guidelines are in place the foundations for repeated success are established.

Just as travelers have relied on the Compass Rose for centuries to utilize the Earth's magnetic field in wayfinding (and as a reminder to this can be found on pretty much every map ever printed), think of your internal compass as a *reminder* of the magnetic forces inside of *you*. In this way *Staying*

True is not some sort of far-reaching achievement, it's natural law.

Just as you don't need to "find" your truth, you don't need to "find" your purpose, you just need to own what's already there.

It comes down to Inquiry. The way to get information from a computer is to press the right combination of keys. Similarly, the way to ensure you are oriented to True North on your path, is to ask the right questions.

When my schoolmate was cornered by bullies, somewhere in my mind the conversation turned to, "Is this right? What am I going to do about it?"

When that famous studio called the question that surfaced was, "Am I being true to myself?"

The more questions you ask of yourself, the surer your step on that journey.

Here's one for you: What is already there that you are not appreciating about yourself? Like when Brendan Bruchard said to me, "Its about time you are here."

What are you not listening to?

What do you need to take in?

Maybe you've been setting your compass to a belief that isn't even true—because you haven't stopped to Inquire Within.

Now is the time to orient yourself to your own True North. Then, set your compass to continually point in that direction.

Some of you might not know, "What the hell is a compass?" I hear you, "How do I set my own compass?"

The first time a compass was crucial to my survival was when I was in the Army ROTC at University of Georgia.

Alone in the woods at 4 am, "What the F am I doing?"

All I needed to do was to find the points they gave me to make it back to base. All you need to do is follow these four points of my method you will find within this book to end up solidly living your truth.

It will be so clear and easy. I've already done the years of hard work.

It's like this, have you ever been to a new city? It's scary you don't know where you should or shouldn't go. I remember one time when I was driving from San Diego to a program on the other side of Los Angeles. I was carrying a barstool and double wide easel in the car. There was no GPS in those days, it was the middle of the night, and I was dangerously low on gas.

I pulled over at the first gas station I could find and the guy at the counter said, "Hey Honey, you better get out of here. Within the next 5 min this is going to turn into a Crips and Blood battle."

I could go no further without gas. I locked myself in the car as I fueled up. Constantly checking over my shoulder and in the mirrors. I was in the car and out of there as soon as the pump stopped. I'm not sure I got the gas cap on before I drove away. One thing is for sure, I did not have a receipt for the expense report the next day.

As I started to drive back to the freeway, the light turned to red. Looking up, I saw two things: 1) No on-ramp back to the freeway and 2) The off-ramp I had exited to get to this gas station was flooded with cars headed in the direction of the gas station I just left.

I didn't know where to go – I was scared. I didn't have anybody to help me get back on course. All I knew was that I could not stay in that spot a moment longer.

It wasn't going to be perfect or follow all the rules, but I was getting out of this situation and back on that freeway—NOW.

"How do I get out of here?"

"What do I know?"

From ROTC training I knew that roads in California run from the freeway East and West and parallel to the freeway within the towns North and South.

"How do I get back on that freeway before all of these cars block the road?"

I was going to have to time my driving to be earlier than them.

"How do I avoid being in the middle of this conflict?"

"Drive!"

I looked left, I looked right, checked the rear-view mirror, took my foot off the break, and pressed the gas while the light was still red. Avoiding a turning car, I went up a few streets and took a left because I knew I was now headed North (parallel to the freeway). I kept my eyes open for major road names. When I came to the first street I recognized for having an exit on the freeway, I took a left. That extra 20-min to get back on track felt like hours, but soon that gas station and its late-night festivities were in my rear-view mirror. A flood of emotion—mostly elation, "I did it!" I turned up the radio and screamed.

What helps get you back on course?

When you are driving in a new city, you constantly reference your phone, "Am I in the right place?" This is the same as consistently asking yourself in life, "Am I being true to myself?" Taking this moment is like pressing pause on a movie, it allows the space to stay on track with your true purpose. The distinction is in honoring the answer you receive when you pose that question. Then, honestly shifting yourself to stay on course. It might not be perfect at first. But, as long as you are heading in the right direction—you'll get there.

For now, hold onto that memory of living your own truth. When you recognize and embrace yourself, you live life on your terms. Rather than trying to fit into someone else's mold or expectations, you radiate in your own skin.

Sure, sometimes, outside factors chip at your resolve. I've lived through some of the darkest hours—financial downfalls, deep emotional and spiritual pain, fractured trust, loss of loved ones, and divorce.

Going down feels like being swallowed by a heavy, unrelenting darkness. It's disorienting. Despair can wrap around you tightly. In isolation, you feel hope is lost. The best way out of any of these challenging times is through it.

Let me say that again, the only way out is through.

Now you want to put the book down, "Now that sucks!"

It's the truth. You have to go through it. I wouldn't have the hunger I do today if it weren't for what I went through. Once you do—you need to celebrate your story. Celebrate yourself.

When women come together at my events and memberships – it is a whole different game. We allow trust and respect for each other while we create the space for people to find their path.

That's what my mission is, to create a community built on love, trust, and respect.

It takes honesty with yourself, discipline and commitment, grit, and self-work to rise above it all and get back to where you feel strong. When you honor the gifts within yourself, it creates a feeling so powerful that, once experienced, it will keep calling you back, again and again. From this place, you do not have to work to make others see your value.

Have you ever had that feeling like I did getting back on that freeway, "YES!" Dance in one place – "I Freaking did that!" "I did the hard!" and it was so much easier than you thought it would be. And if you haven't you should do it now.

When I went for my ROTC scholarship, I got to the point where I said, "Y'all, I'm doing this."

Stepping into that program was crossing an uncharted frontier. Let's put it this way, I was the only sorority girl there. I was fully aware of the space I was entering. I would slip out of my floral Laura Ashely dress and into my fatigues. The stares lingered and the expectations were heavier. In that uniform there were moments of pride and doubt.

The pressure I put on myself to exceed expectations was overwhelming. It was grueling, hard-fought, and deeply rewarding. In the end, I was proud to be a part of something bigger than myself and to have contributed with my parents towards financing my degree.

Among the many items that crossed my path during these adventures was a large illustrated poster depicting a wildish woman. It hung in my mom's bathroom of all places. The wild woman in the poster was balancing towering wands, surrounded by wolves and stars, all leading to a bright yellow open door with a lit candle inside. The borders as well as the design were tribal and intriguing. It left me with a sense of wonder and intrigue. The essence of its power has stayed with me for life.

Every time I went into my mom's room I would stare at it. I could feel the aura of that woman's audacious free spirit. Who was she to be so bold? So free and so gorgeous? I imagined myself living by her example. What could I do with so much life inside that it spilled out at the seams? Her vibrance danced her off the paper and into my bones, and over time, she sculpted core guiding principles straight into my heart. As I practiced the wisdom her art taught me, I found—my own *resolutions* about what it means to *stay true*. This is how I see her; it is also how I see *you*.

I believe that...

When you OWN IT, "they" see it as you walk into a room. You are the "real" thing. Your True North is simply to be you, all of you.

4

INQUIRY & IDENTITY: FIND YOUR WAY

**How many people have told you "Your way?"
People have said you *"can't"* or that you
"should" – how do they know?
It's not their baby.**

One day, I was walking through the living room and found Joel Olsten on tv. He was telling a story from the Bible about Zechariah and his wife, Elizabeth.

Zechariah was a Jewish high priest. Both husband and wife were very old and had never been able to have children. An angel Gabriel appeared to

Zechariah letting him know that he and Elizabeth were going to have a baby and that they were to name him John.

There were all of these challenges with the name John. In the Jewish faith often, you name the baby in some way after a deceased relative. "John" didn't make sense to anyone else in their congregation. Joel's story talked about how Elizabeth had to keep overcoming objections to her name choice.

G-d had a plan for little baby John, he grew up to be John the Baptist, the man who baptized Jesus.

Joel Olsten's moral of the story was: "Don't let anyone name your baby!"

You and only you have the connection to your TRUTH. Everyone on the outside is a character of the story, but only you know what is right for your baby (and your life).

Read the title again. It says, "Find your way."

Whether off track from fear, distraction, or simply feeling overwhelmed by life's challenges, The Compass Rose is a framework to recalibrate and navigate your way back.

In order to find yourself metaphorically in life or physically on a map—you have to clearly define where you are. Think of the mall map, "You are here."

What happens when you look at your position on that map and don't like what you see? What if all the voices around you and the noise of society are insisting you are in the right place, yet everything inside you tells otherwise?

At a program I facilitate, people climb a 60 ft telephone pole as a metaphor. Some people climb the pole to celebrate. Some people use it to break through their fears. Some people do it just because it is there and part of the program.

The goal is for you to celebrate along the way. There is another element where people are given an option to accept a trapeze challenge. Before a person leaps to accept the challenge, I ask them to ask themselves, "Is that your trapeze?"

In life, the trapeze could be your next big goal. College, a job, marriage...

 Since the time he was six years old, Jos heard me ask thousands of people climbing the pole, "Is that your trapeze?"

Jos came home from his first year of college and said, "Mom, that's not my trapeze." How many people have gone for the trapeze because you thought that's what you *should* do?

Jos found the clearest language he could find to communicate to me his location on the map. With those words, I knew that college was not right for him. This was not his way.

So many people define this time in a young adult's life as "the college years." That looks like a traditional 4-year program followed by a master's degree, followed by student loans. Remember the story about not letting them name your baby? This was not Jos's baby's name.

As a result of this self-awareness, Jos course-corrected his plan and became a student in the Gemological Institute of America's Graduate Gemologist program. It was a big risk, but it felt right. There are no student loans for GIA students.

I had to come up with all the money. I had to come up with an apartment and the rent in New York City. It cost $5000 a month for him to live in Manhattan. Students late two days in a semester to class, are excused from the program.

Then, it happened during his first week—the sub-way was late. Just like that, with one tardy, we were already committed.

He had no experience going into the program; but, he was passionate about the results. This is an intensive course study, five flunked out and yet Jos graduated with a perfect score in 2017.

In massive momentum for three years, he began building a name for himself in NYC and then, COVID happened. I like to call this "the mandatory pause." Talk about a lot of "noise" to navigate through. I'm sure you know one of these people. Were you one?

After "being made by my Mom to flee New York for Las Vegas," as Jos says, he paused and took time for Inquiry to question himself and find that True North, "What should I do now?" He bounced around Central America during COVID.

He says, "I had an amazing time learning about myself and what makes ME happy—and how I operate."

Like Jos, you are going to get off course when life throw sh*t out that is of your control at you.

Jos did all he needed to do—he stopped. He knew it was all there within him. He went on a discovery process. He went deep. He did the work.

When the pandemic ended, he found himself in the Midwest selling roofs. Knowing roofing wasn't his gig, with plans to retreat back to Nicaragua, he stopped into a jewelry shop to collect a watch he had won.

He calls this moment, "The Spark."

I received his call, "Mom, tucked away in the middle of Minnesota, I found one of the best jewelry stores in all of America!"

Imagine my Graduate Gemologist's joy after selling roofs, to be surrounded again by cases of every rare gem imaginable.

He said, "Mom, this is it. It's the place I've been hoping to find. The staff is impeccable!"

To this day Jos says, "What I've learned from my mom is that G-d has your back. The best decision I ever made has been to trust that "guided feeling.""

Have you had a time in your life when you ignored the "nudge from the universe?" When you didn't trust your intuition?

Have you made a decision in life based on what you thought you "*should*" do?

Have you ever found yourself having to course correct while enduring pain and frustration that could have been avoided had you only trusted that "guided feeling" or your own initial gut instinct?

A man I know got married because all he ever wanted in life was to be a Dad. How many of you know people who have gotten married because it was the "right time" not necessarily the "right person?"

On the night of his engagement, this man drove his fiancé to his parents' house to announce the happy news. The couple walked into a living room-filled with loving, familiar faces exclaiming, "We're engaged!" And received a quiet-less-than-excited, "Oh! You are?!" Before a fumbled, "Congratulations! We are so happy for you guys!"

On his wedding day, walking around the gardens where the ceremony was about to take place, the groom's brother-in-law said, "You know, it's not too late."

This man had dated quite a bit in high school, but had gone through college without so much as even a date. He was so happy to have a girl interested in spending time with him and the timing was right. This is when he "should" get married—he thought, "This must be the one?"

After all, the timing was right. He had calculated his entire life. If he was going to have kids by this date and grandchildren by this date, she should be "the one."

There were moments when emotions flashed hot, "That's not the way I was raised." He thought, "How will she be a patient and loving mother with a temper like that?" Or when she partied too hard and flirted with other men. He thought, "Is she really mature enough to commit my life to?" A quiet voice inside wondered, "Is this really the right one for me?" A solid, silent, empty pang to the chest responded.

Yet, he released these doubts and physical warnings to, "Well, maybe that's the journey of marriage? Growing old together means growing through tough times as well as happy. Maybe patience, commitment, and responsibility are the lessons we will be learning together as a couple?"

Fast-forward 20 years—a proud father of two, nightly lying in bed with tears streaming uncontrollably, clutching his pillow, praying through the pain for any sense of relief. Feeling lonely and isolated, all while sharing a bed and life with someone consumed by rage, addiction, and infidelity.

He felt like a prisoner of his own thoughts. What began as a faint pang of doubt in his heart whenever he questioned, "Is this right?" had now grown unbearable. Echoing louder with each passing day was the knowing that this pain came from doing what he "*should*" and not trusting his intuition.

Have you ever ignored that inner voice nudging you to take a different course of action? Perhaps you ignored very logical advice offered by well-intentioned, respected loved-ones like the brother-in-law in the story.

I am a smart person with a lot of great experiences and I still have ignored my own instincts. When I've found myself there—I say, "G-d Loren, you knew different!"

And at the height of it all, when you find yourself in the depths of self-loathing, "because you knew better!" you have two choices. Stay there or take action.

Moments like this have epic Momma Bear potential. Have you ever found yourself in a momma-bear kind of moment? Momma-bears stand at nothing to protect their den. There are few creatures on Earth who would survive once a Momma-bear feels her cubs are threatened. A Momma-bear Moment is when you stop crying and hugging your pillow and realize it is up to you to become the hero in your own story.

You decide, "That is enough!" You put both feet firmly under you and take action, because you have no control over the past and the future depends on this moment NOW. And that, you can OWN!

Your badass and beautiful woman journey begins when you ground yourself in the certainty of truth you've defined solidly for yourself. When you listen to the beat of your own heart. When you start asking yourself questions and truly listening for the answers.

And please note: This is where your life makes a major pivot—if you really create this awareness. This is a line in the sand. In order to move forward, you have to see both yourself and your life clearly. You need to know exactly who you are and where you want to go. No one else will tell you to move forward. No one else's opinion even matters. No one is coming to save you. You have to participate in your own rescue. Frankly there isn't enough time to wait for permission.

If you need it, one badass and beautiful woman to another, this is your permission slip. *This* is the point where you get to shine and actually *live*. Allow me to save you the head- and heart-ache of waiting to trust yourself. Let this be your burn the boats, throw everything out the window *except for the truth inside* moment.

Please tell me you're with me.

When maybes become musts in order for you to thrive, clarity shines its light of transparency on the mess of life's decisions. A deep precision rises up as you step to the edge of all previously held limits. This is the kind of clarity I found while raising my youngest child and only daughter, Asher—especially in her early years.

From the moment I found out I was carrying her; she became a bright (and beautifully wild) part of my badass and beautiful journey. We had just moved to Las Vegas from Portland because my youngest son, Quinn, was suffering from severe mold allergies. Determined to use the transition as a new chapter, I told myself I was going to "get in shape" and start some needed new fitness rituals. At 42 years old, I was ready for both a geographical and personal reset.

And... a reset is exactly what I got—just not exactly the one I had envisioned.

I did, in fact, "get in shape"—a very round shape, that is. I found out that I was pregnant just a few weeks into the move... and quickly discovered that being pregnant in my 40s was quite a bit different than when I'd had my first two sons, six and ten years earlier respectively.

My first two ultrasounds indicated that the pregnancy was 100 percent normal. The doctors believed a third ultrasound would not be unnecessary, as these are reserved for pregnancies deemed "high-risk," and mine hadn't made that qualification. Yet – I had a nagging feeling. A voice inside was pushing me, "*ask for the third ultrasound.*" Thankfully, I listened.

It turned out that blood was not getting to the placenta, and Asher was not receiving any nutrients. I was going to have to get her out of me and into the world right away.

The challenge? My life was still in transition. Our insurance hadn't transferred to Nevada yet. I only had medical coverage back in Oregon. So, I booked a flight and flew to Portland the very next day. From there, everything moved at an astounding, constant-snow-ball-of-change pace.

With urgency and without any more advance warning, seventeen years ago, on June 29, 2007, (*in case you are ever on a game show the same day as Disney's "Ratatouille" and the first iphone came out*), one day after my flight and two days post the ultrasound no one thought I needed, Asher made her grand entrance into the world.

She was a teeny, tiny, precious being... who snored like an extended freight train; which, gave me pause. I was worried there might be something wrong with her. Friends and doctors kept advising me she'd grow out of it. In spite of the nagging pulling in my gut and sleepless nights haunting her crib, I let sleeping beauty—snooze.

It took me years to "catch myself." What I mean is, really listen to my inner knowing, my voice inside. Finally, the moment arrived when my soul awoke. I reached my threshold and took her to an Ear, Nose and Throat specialist.

Well beyond my first inclination that something about her snoring *"wasn't quite right,"* this specialist explained that Asher's adenoids were enlarged, which was making it hard for her to breathe. Immediately, the simple surgery was scheduled.

Following this incident, the Mommy-guilt was real, I felt horrible. How could I let my beautiful girl down? What kind of an example was I setting for my daughter? How and why did I ignore my own intuition? My poor baby had suffered unnecessarily for *years*.

Then a few years later, there was the divorce. At this point, Asher was four, and my boys were 10 and 14. It is safe to report that Asher had her own weather pattern during this time. Divorces are hard on the entire family. Kids act out more than "use their words" in times of stress. I summed up her "cranky" and "hard to please" temperament to be the way she was "working through her feelings." Friends around me at the time reinforced the story I was telling myself. As I would return from soothing her tempests, everyone around us would assure me, "Some kids are just cranky."

Meanwhile, everything in my life seemed to be compounding from all angles. In the throes of divorce, there is no space to press pause and get perspective. On one hand, navigating lawyers and the legalities of parenting plans while leveraging assets and confronting financial insecurities was like taking an ocean wave in the face, head-on. In another corner, decades-long relationships and beliefs were in continuous stages of break-down. With three children, actively making day-to-day life and happily ever-after dreams happen through pure faith in the spirit of abundance was a 24-7 intentional practice of conscious discipline. Ultimately, I was riding the stages of grief like an overpriced and uncoordinated group workout. Divorce stretched the parent paper thin. Long story short, my brain and heart were in a survival mode trance.

Then, I woke up. One day, Asher came home from preschool with a note from her school attached to her backpack that read: "Take your daughter to the optometrist *immediately*."

"Me?! Daughter to the Optometrist?! My Dad was an Optometrist?! Why do I need to take her there?"

My little ball-of-fire was the catalyst to shat-ter my hypnotic divorcee-state. Daughter to Mother, Sister to Sister, Friend to Friend – there is something primal that rocks the soul when another woman needs you. Especially, when that woman is your little one. She was seen immediately.

We found out Asher was suffering from what some would call impaired vision – in fact she couldn't see. In fact, she was nearly blind. What's more—once her struggle to *see* went away, so did her temper tantrums.

As the daughter of an optometrist (trust me, the irony was not lost on me), the lesson stung doubly.

In truth, I felt like my Dad might be reaching out to share some parenting wisdom from "the other side": "*Pause Loren—listen to your own truth.*"

Here lies the title of this chapter. To reset back to your True North, your core *identity*, you have to stop and *find your way*. You have to pause and look around.

The Inquiry can look like this:

"Who am I right now?"

"What am I doing?

"Wait, this is not who I am!"

If the world doesn't give it to you, make the space to ask and truly notice (**see**) the details. From this point on, just as Asher could now see clearer physically, my inner vision would no longer be clouded by fear, doubt, insecurities, or outside influences—all I needed to provide these kids was *within me*.

I regularly share this core moment at my events. Often, when we're cranky about where we're at in our lives, it's not because of what seems to be happening *to* us; but, because we perceive we are unable to step back to see the big picture. When our vision of the future is impaired or we are unable to focus with clarity on what we want in/for our lives—a part of us is closed off to life. This all comes down to how you see and therefore relate to yourself and your *identity*.

I often say that I like my content to be all-encompassing and easy to digest, learn, and then apply to your life. I call it the "Attention all K-Mart Shoppers" approach. To help us understand in the most simple terms, *identity* – I'm going to give you some information I picked up from Sesame Street.

Well, actually a study done in conjunction with the University of Chicago for Sesame Street, but close enough.

The study shares that one of the most influential parts of development is a child's sense of *identity*. Greater self-esteem and pride stems from a positive self-*identity*.

But, what is *identity*?

That sounds like an existential question. Thank God, it is not really that difficult to answer.

Identity is the "Where have you been?" and "Where are you now?" kind of questions. "Who do you want to be?" "Who are you becoming?" "How do you see yourself in the world?" You might have a past *identity*, but the most power is in the who you are becoming.

Disney's "Inside Out 2" does a great job of showing the core memories that collect into threads of thoughts growing from your stream of consciousness and ultimately produce themselves as a sculpture of self in the center of the brain. These core beliefs form *identity* and from that place all other decisions are made. When anxiety takes over, it works for a while—but eventually, it's a colossal mess. The main character forgets her core belief of "I am a good person" and briefly believes, "I'm not good enough." It takes unbottling all of the emotions and allowing Joy to take the controls for the hero to "make the team" and thrive.

Who was there for your up-bringing? Who were your role models? It could be regional—many locations on the globe have people who stand for something or have a similar way of handling challenges. For instance, in New Hampshire people live by the motto, "Live free or die." People in Australia have something called "Tall Poppy Syndrome" which is a collective *identity* that keeps an individual's focus on being humble contributors to the whole.

Core aspects of *identity* include gender and roles you play within your community and family. Beliefs, morals, religion, and philosophies are all factored into *identity*. External factors such as height, weight, age, and socioeconomics are also factored into "*identity*."

In the words of "The Who" song from the 1970s, "*identity*" is, "Who are you?" This is where you name your baby.

The one that is most important is not about where you are from – and all that – it is who are you going to and not going to claim now? Like Jos knew that was not his trapeze.

What are those parts of you that shape every-thing you do moving forward? They might have served you until that point.

Here is an example: Back to when I first started dating my husband, Z, I told him straight-up, "I'm the catch of the century."

He laughed when I said it, but I doubled-back, "No, I'm serious. I'm the *absolute* catch of the century."

I meant it, and after I said it twice—he knew it and... that's how he treats me. This may sound like a brazen, egotistical thing to say, but if I didn't claim and express my truth which is my *identity*, why would he?

Your *identity* is your personal truth; it's who you *think* you are at the core. Like we said, questions activate the magnet that pulls us to the North Star which is your *identity*. Think of , *questions* as the core tool that shapes (like that diamond) our *identity*. Questions determine our entire thinking process. They are the tool we use to create mean-ing. They guide and navigate decisions. Most importantly, questions dictate how we choose a course of action. They inform our next steps and give clarity. In this way, questions dictate how we experience life.

When you ask yourself, "Am I staying true?" and really listen, the answer calls back with a steadfast certainty in your gut. Like that man who asked himself if this was the right person for him. He received a physical response. He ignored it, but it was there.

There's no denying your own truth. You don't need a 360-analysis or a board of directors to weigh in. You just know.

My son, Quinn, says I would run through a brick wall in the name of "what is true."

Truth doesn't mind being questioned. When it's true, it's calming, peaceful, and simultaneously rock solid. Your truth is bullet-proof. Like Jos when he needed to become a Gradate Gemologist or the man who married because he thought he *should*, truth isn't just a privilege or a luxury, living in truth is imperative for your healthy existence.

Collectively on this planet, we are unraveling, numb and unable to see a better future. We live in a world that's become so disassociated to authentic nature that we've become a bit zombie-like. I believe that it's actually our role in humanity to step into our truth, our power. This gift is not only for our own benefit; it's a present that we leave for future generations.

Here's something, you have a choice to show up and play small—or show up and be badass and beautiful. Sometimes, we elect to "play small" in order to fit in. But, what if we brought it all?

A Psi Chi Journal of Psychological Research published a University of Virginia at Wise study of first year college students. The study found that there are two parts to *identity* development: Exploration and Commitment.

Questions are Exploration phase (which can serve as the great reset). One little question can change everything and snap you back to True North.

Quinn has always felt like the way I bring questions to him allows him to feel set up to "take risks." That's an interesting thought. What good comes from taking a risk? Risks are the reason we have most anything worth having on this planet from chocolate to cars. Who was the first person who decided to taste watermelon? What happened when people in Europe wondered what was on the other side of the ocean? Power comes from Inquiry. Revolutions happen when people start questioning.

The Inquiry or questions you ask yourself steer your feet and open your eyes to possibility. This affects your level of experience, which opens up your "scope" or view of a situation.

Your perspective is your reality. Quinn says Inquiry is what helps you peel back the onion on your life decisions.

Use this to your advantage to serve your truth. But beware, you may have to employ a course correction. It is critical to catch yourself in the blitz. This means to awaken a fresh mind and a thoughtful pause.

"What else could be true?"

"Is this congruent with who am I?"

"Is this congruent with who I *want* to be?"

"Am I living *my* truth?"

Identity Exploration and Commitment happens at all different times of life. But I hear stories all the time of young women who head off to college or camp and connect with an initial "friend group," only to find themselves lonely and in a personal "struggle."

For many, I believe those first few years of college can feel like a dark night for the soul until this commitment of true *identity* shines its light.

Here's an actual example: When my friend's daughter left for school, she was very excited to have an "instant friend group." Back when I went to college, who you ended up with as a roommate your first year was a little more like a 180-day blind date, but now—college students are lucky to have "social media" as a first-look into your soon-to-be roomie's life.

Over the months, my friend's daughter became more and more excited as she realized her new roommate's high school friend group seemed to be coming to their school en-masse!

"Mom! Mom! I will have so many friends on the first day of school! Isn't that great!?"

We all celebrated with her.

Half-way through the year, my friend's daughter called in tears. She was desperately lonely and couldn't figure out why. With all of the people around her, she still felt like she was alone standing in a crowded room. On one hand, she had a friend for every occasion... except for when she really needed someone. The more time went by, the more "fair-weather" her instant-friend group seemed.

Alone in the dorm, battling a 103-degree fever, while everyone else went out to a big party—despite her having played nurse for several of them with the same illness just a week before. Then, there was the night they all got bored at a party. She had been chatting with someone from her class when she realized her friend group had vanished. She searched every floor of the fraternity house, but they were gone, leaving her to walk home in the dark, alone. The next morning, they teased her, "You're so crazy! Why do you always insist on walking home by yourself?"

Conversations became difficult for my friend's daughter with this friend group. She was a very well-informed and world-conscious soul who tasked herself on being aware of global events. When she would bring up a topic to one of her "friends" she would find herself getting the response, "What are you even talking about?" or "I don't know—who even cares?" My friend's daughter started to change her own conversations and behaviors to try to "fit in." With each month, my friend's daughter became more and more lonely. Her grades waivered.

Finally, an intervention was needed.

My friend pointed out to her daughter, "You are a Peacemaker. You are changing yourself to 'fit in.' At this point you are volunteering for pain. If you are not able to spend your days talking about things you love and enjoy—you will never truly find your tribe. It might hurt or feel scary to let go of what does not serve you, but ultimately—you will thrive."

My friend's daughter learned the consequences of not speaking her truth, but not before fully hitting the deepest, darkest moments of lonely. She went three-years feeling like an outsider. Ultimately, she arrived at the moment when nothing else mattered.

She had to fully surrender to the realization that if she had to "wear the mask" of something she is not, these people were not her people. She would not let them name her baby. This was not her trapeze. This was not her way.

Letting go of what no longer aligned with her truth was essential for her to embrace what truly mattered and re-direct herself to what mattered most.

The result? The acceptance she found with the group of friends in her senior year—those who embraced her for her authentic self—became the greatest gift of all: a sense of belonging. As Asher would say, "They loved her for all the parts of her whole."

How many people do you know who might have experienced that in school? Do you know someone with a similar story? Might you still be trying to "fit in" with a crowd incongruent with your truth?

Back to my motherhood reckoning with Asher (and let this be a message you remember)—You can't see your own truth, nor the truth of a situation, if you're vision is impaired. Success lies in delineating between power-based and fear-based self-inquiry.

In fact, when Asher was just a year old, I decided to take a long-awaited trip to Malawi that I'd planned. The same year, I ran the Alaskan marathon. All my friends told me I was crazy. People told me that I should wait until my kids were older to do such "big" things.

There were parts of me that started to listen. "The Noise" was trying to creep in. And I had to catch myself. I had to keep going back to it. You need to go back to the anchors. Nope. I'm *staying true* to myself and doing this.

Fortunately, I never listened. I asked myself a different question, "What would happen if I don't do this? What will I miss? What will my kids miss out on? How do I want my kids to remember this moment? What brings me the most pride – having accomplished this or waited?"

I decided that I need to live life *now*.

I decided that the mother my kids needed and that I wanted to be is one that lives each day as an example of what is possible in this life. I wanted them to be inspired to create and follow their own vision, manifest and realize their own greatest potential.

It turns out, that was my window of opportunity for these things. Now, in hindsight, if I had let them name my baby, I would have never done these things. That Alaska Marathon is a one-of-a-kind, no sh*t marathon. If I had listened to the advice of others and missed those chances, I would have never run that marathon (one of the greatest personal achievements of my life).

I decided that tomorrow is not a promise. Waiting was not an option for me. I didn't care what anyone else thought about my vision, I was going for it, no matter what. That was my trapeze.

I'm not the only one.

Dr. Seuss (Theodore Geisel)'s first book was rejected by 27 publishers.

It took JK Rowling 7 years to write her first Harry Potter novel. While she was broke and living off welfare, the book was initially rejected by 12 publishers.

Walt Disney was fired from his first editorial job at a newspaper because he "lacked imagination and had no good ideas."

Katy Perry's first record label went out of business. Then she was dropped by two more labels until she had her first hit ten years later.

Sigmund Freud was actually booed off the platform in his first public speech, and amazingly Michael Jordan was cut from his high school basketball team.

This reminds me of that video for Steve Jobs, "Here's to the crazy ones..." Frida Kahlo said it this way, *They will call you "crazy" because you are, because you were born with the gift of seeing things differently and that scares them.*

They're going to call you "intense" because you are, because you were born with the value well placed to allow yourself to feel it all fully and that intimidates them.

They're going to call you "selfish" because that's right, because you found out that you're the most important thing in your life and that doesn't suit them.

You're going to be called in many ways, with many judgments, for a long time, but stay firm on yourself and what you want, and I promise you one day they're going to call you to say, "thank you for existing.""

Other people's opinions don't matter. But, what you think and align yourself with energetically does matter. This ties into a major operating principle that I believe guides your *identity*—A Theory of *Archetypes*. Archetypes are a way to clearly and specifically communicate and visualize yourself as you wish to be.

In that moment when Jos knew college wasn't the right place for him. That was clear. But, then we had to define who he wanted to be and where he needed to go to make that happen. Archetypes help with this clarity.

I was inspired about these by Carolyn Myss almost 36 years ago. Some of them are not pretty. Such as the prostitute—how many times have you embraced that "sell out" archetype? You have to be careful of which archetypes you embrace.

Archetypes are, "an original pattern from which all things remain the same." In Psychology, Archetypes can be referred to as a "collective memory" and are found in every species. In fact, Carl Yung had a theory that Archetypes are passed from generation to generation. In writing fiction, Archetypes are a tool used by writers of fiction. Common themes in human characteristics were observed over generations of story-telling. These commonalities have been grouped together and developed under common characters through-out history to help express feelings, emotions, and in general: identities of fictional characters for movies and books.

For female roles, archetypes often include: the Lover, the Maiden, the Huntress (or Amazon), the Sage, the Mystic, the Mother, and the Queen.

Think of famous fictional characters from movies that take on these archetypes. Wonderwoman is the "Amazon." The "Sage" is Harmonie Granger or Belle from Beauty and the Beast. Snow White was the ultimate "Mother" for the Seven Dwarfs. Dorothy from the Wizard of Oz is a "Maiden."

How are you feeling as we are talking about these? Are you already making the assumption you are not... the... not the... are you making judgements of what these even mean? Imagine if you were the queen just for a second.

Even in the story arch of fictional characters, there are moments when like a kaleidoscope, multiple personas present. To expose the beauty of the feminine, it is important to note that inside every one of us are all of the archetypes in varying capacities.

"Different times call for different measures." This is an old-fashioned term from reading sheet music that relates to this thought well—varied life experiences call for different energies to be brought forth within us. To exaggerate, you wouldn't show up for a job interview in the same way you show up for a night out on the town with friends.

In cinema or books, you see only a few dimensions of a human. In "real-life" the archetypes are all within each of us to be pulled forth in order to fully express and therefore experience life. Within us, we contain the Warrior, the Poet, the Hunter, the Shaman, the Creator, the Destroyer, the Prostitute, the Barbie, the Healer, the Comic, the Magician, the Starborn, the Storm, the Shadow, and the Mystic.

Each and every combination is unique and dynamic. Some aspects of self are based on chapters and life-experiences. Our complexity cannot be reduced down or compared to any other living human being. Our truth, our *self*, is ours and ours alone. Like those diamonds, no other person contains the expression we possess.

Only you can fully know, appreciate and share the exact amount of each ingredient or archetype within you. But you'll only be able to share it if you first acknowledge and *honor* each part. To do otherwise is to become lost in the maze of outward expectations.

Looking at my own life experiences as examples, back when that boy was threatening my schoolmate, my Amazonian warrior-goddess surfaced. On the day when my son graduated from GIA, the proud Mother was present. On the day I walked down the aisle to meet my husband, I could feel the Queen within me hold her head high.

Are you stuck somewhere or know someone, feeling exhausted, asking unproductive questions like, "What am I doing wrong?" or like my friend's daughter, "Why am I so alone?" If so, more than likely there are parts of life that you don't *see*. Parts of *yourself* you haven't noticed or even discovered. Is there a perspective you can take to see more clearly the situations you are volunteering yourself to be apart?

Most people stifle or quiet at least one archetype. Perhaps—the softer self, maybe the adventurous self, or even more often, we dismiss the regal, noble and deserving self.

Remember when you were a girl and you would sit back and think, "When I grow up, I am going to handle this situation...." In day-dreams you would "take care of business" in your mind, planning for how you would conduct yourself when it would one-day be "your turn to be in charge."

Which archetype would you say was present in those scenarios? Would you say one showed up more than another? Who?

With this intention of playing full-out, it brings to mind for me the Greek, Roman, Norse, Celtic, Native American, and Egyptian traditions of high priestesses and goddesses. Talk about attributes we could each want to "grow up to be." For this reason, at events, I often relate the archetype conversation for women to goddesses:

- The Mother = Demeter Archetype (nurturing)
- The Maiden = Persephone Archetype (attentive)
- The Huntress = Artemis Archetype (fierce)

- The Mystic = Hestia Archetype (the fire that sustains life)
- The Sage = Athena Archetype (wisdom)
- The Queen = Hera Archetype (noble)
- The Lover = Aphrodite Archetype (unconditional love)

Maybe your "goddesses" aren't those listed above. Perhaps you can find inspiration with these: Frigg (clairvoyance), Cybele (wild), Brigid (healing), Elpis (hope), Freya (beauty), Enyo (destruction), Macha (life), Gaia (Earth), Harmonia (harmony), Iris (messenger), Sedna (sea), Mania (craze), Anuket (prosperity), and Nike (victorious).

Doesn't this sound like fun?! Don't you want to go out and get a costume? Who wants to own this!?

Every Halloween, my costume was Cat Woman. To some she is scary. To me, she represents a mystic, feminine empowerment, and sensuality. Batman's main love interest, she is a complex character—the ultimate example of Badass & Beautiful. For me she is based on the duality of all women. She is rooted in the Egyptian goddess Bast. She goes out of her way to avoid harming the innocent and also avoids killing. She makes it happen from behind her mask.

Our friend Lee, the Wonder Woman, totally owns this. She always shows up with a smile willing to take on every challenge, leaping design outcomes with a single-bound with laser focus for our team because she totally claims her archetypes. In fact, she has created an archetype course we include in our events and is my Lead Trainer on my Manifest Your _____ Course (which also includes this philosophy).

Lee tells the story that after her divorce, she felt the calling to do more, to be more for herself and for her children. With a heart full of compassion and a determined spirit, she summoned the grace of her warrior (Wonder Woman).

Lee chooses a new archetype every year, embodying the attributes into her manifestation journey. She dawns the crown of the sovereign queen, she waves the wand of Aphrodite, she gives gifts of Mermaid tears. And it has big effects! She is Australian and has provided her two school-aged kids two US cross-country adventures within a year.

Lee faces challenges head on. She knows when to lead and when to listen. She is authentic and unwavering in her dedication. Lee lifts others up along the way. Like anyone, she has her moments of doubt, but she will say out-loud and to others, "Straighten your crown Wonder Woman—Let's do this!" And we do. Her track record is so consistent for results that we have a saying, "#LeaveItToLee."

Take a moment and think of times when you can remember some of the archetypes mentioned so far in your own life. Think of times when it would have helped a situation had you allowed a different archetype to be present. Think of the kind of leader and collaborator you could be if you embraced archetypes with the same zeal as Lee.

This might seem like fun-and-games; however, archetypes are a tool you can apply to your life to help you show up as your true self. When something is defined—it is difficult to ignore. Empower yourself with the intention of a persona! Take the time to realize the unique combination of personal aspects within you and using this archetype philosophy to put a name and intention her.

I challenge you to have fun with this. Just as a kaleidoscope can create an entirely new pattern with a single click, every human represents a unique combination of elements, experiences and qualities. If you do not align with the thought of being a goddess, find your own creative titles.

Are you a Badass and Beautiful Businesswoman? A Sexy Soulmate? A Wealth Wizard? A Stud(ette) Athlete? A Badass Warrior? A Trail Blazer? A Sizzling Artist? A Mesmerizing Creator? A Momma Bear? A Pioneer Woman? An Explorer? A Magical Witch Doctor Healer? A Wild Woman?

I've been calling myself a *Fit Foxy Vixen* for well over 30-years. This one consistent reminder brings me back to a mindset empowering me to be my most powerful self.

Many studies have proven – and most recently, a 2021 study in Japan, showed that the activity of writing things down helps people commit things to memory more firmly. With this knowledge in mind, I write it down, say it out-loud, post it on my computer, and reinforce it in my mind over and over again throughout the day and week. This practice has pulled me through re-claiming my body post-partum three times and menopause.

It doesn't matter how young you are, how many times you've tried and not succeeded, how tired you are or how old you are—you can still claim an empowering and more congruent *identity*.

Your brain is actually pre-wired for victory. It is called Neuroplasticity. There are pathways to success in your brain. They may not be firmly fully open yet—but they exist. You only have to begin the activity and the rewards will be yours. Once your brain gets used to this "success connection" it covers that bond in the brain with myelin. Likewise, when you don't use something, the brain "prunes" that connection. Sort of like when they send the memories to the "back of the mind" in "Inside Out 2." Moral of the story – if you don't want to lose it—USE IT!

Have you heard of Iris Apfel? If I could show you her picture, you'd probably know who I'm talking about. She passed away at 102-years-old, a fashionista with a designer clothing line and a rug line. She was a rare, funky, gypsy bird of pure life, who made a point to celebrate life daily. When you looked at her, you could see it. She was funky, quirky, colorful, real and true. She still is one of my goal Archetypes.

Actually, Iris reminded me a lot of my mom. All of the things that, at one time, I thought she was weird and wacky about. I used to roll my eyes at my mom because she never fit in. I get it now.

What about you? Are you ready to step up and step into your power? I encourage you to notice the archetypes within yourself now. Once you own who you *really* are, the question, "Am I staying true?" gains an entirely new and poignant power.

It is important to note another dimension of this concept. Sometimes, we hide behind traits that seem more powerful or strong as a protection mechanism. In this way, we wear proverbial "masks" in order to cover up parts of ourselves that we don't want others to see. Often, I observe people hiding more tender, softer sides. Much like my friend's daughter did with her "instant friend group" in college.

My Aunt Lee used to own an art store. When I was a little girl, I remember going in, browsing around, looking at all of the different mediums for artistic potential. For some reason, the plaster molds would often hold my attention. I'd stop and look at the form taken by one shape to create another and think to myself, "Everyone wants to fit into the mold. That's what everyone is trying to do."

As my friend's daughter learned, we have to take off the plaster and stop "fitting in."

It seems even more challenging with social media in the mix. There is duality with social media. On one side, we are more connected to friends and family than any other generation because we never have a reason to lose touch. However, if there was a friend group you might have passed time with when you were not in your truth, you may be tempted to live up to the expectations you set for yourself with others "back then"—even if this is not YOU.

In the process, I see people "should" all over themselves. Creating content that attracts the eye of everyone. Because, when it comes down to it— we are all looking for connection. The reason we wear masks at all is to attract more humans.

Here is a tool I have begun using to "smash the masks" on social. I think of social media as an extension of my Manifestation Board. A daily expression of the places I am sending my energy in order to achieve my outcomes. I am selective in my "digital space" just as I am of my space in real life.

Examples? Here is an easy one. I facilitate health programs. I know what it takes to have the mind, body, and whole package I dream for myself. At different times in my life, I needed to motivate myself to have the discipline to drink that water, walk those steps, attend the classes, and visit the sauna. During those times my posts would have been everything from doctor's findings about hydration and the benefits of saunas to new work-outs that you can integrate into your daily dog walk. Incantations that I would say when I woke up in the morning to keep my energy up. Classes run by friends that I wanted to check out in the area (hoping I would get some friends to join for accountability). This makes social media a part of the ritual to being true to you.

Nobody wants to be alone. And the antidote to being lonely is to be you. It takes energy to *try* to be something we are not. Most of us role-play. We take on identities we think we're "supposed" to fulfill. We look outward for clues about what success should look like and embody character traits that others seem to appreciate.

Instead of posting for other people, I am posting for myself daily. What will serve us best is if we together, break the mold—for both ourselves and others. Said another way, let's stop trying fit (and put) each other in boxes. Pre-defined boxes are too small to contain the truth of our unique spirits. When I make a post it is feeding my passion and fueling the momentum I need to continue to achieve small wins on the way to my vision for myself.

Whether you put *yourself* into a box or someone else put you there, it's time to step out. It's time to break free. The greatest gift we can give each other, and therefore, the world, is to first *stay true*—to live *out loud*—and then... to lift each other up. Life is about *living* every minute, out loud. Please don't be afraid to play BIG. We need you, all of you, in this world.

In truth, I have found, people's personalities are dynamic and multi-dimensional. What I have observed through my work is that all women are comprised of multiple layers and multiple corresponding expressions. Fact is always better than fiction, but one thing we can borrow from the world's best fiction writers to help learn more about the complexity of our own human spirit is character development. Because, aren't we all our own "main characters" after-all?

In the attempt to fit in with perceived expectations, we put on the "mask" that we perceive will best fit the situation. Thinking the assumed one archetype will protect or find us favor. Most commonly, we end up feeling fatigued and lost because we are literally covering our truth in order to play a form of "dress-up." Often, several masks are piled on top of each other.

The 2023 "Barbie" movie has a scene that addresses this practice that results from women's perceived mantle of social obligation. In a mono-logue, a character addresses a crowd with these sentiments. She laments that there is a silent code of contradiction that as a woman you have to show up as enough, best-in-show, and an equal-to-all-others all at the same time. Also, powerful and not, as well as intelligent, but not.

This scene from the movie is the perfect depiction of the source of fatigue I've observed time and again. It is important to realize that in a roomful of people—we could potentially be operating within a roomful of other masked humans. Within the layers, there are the expectations of masks, the actual masks, the masks from social media, and the effects of colliding masks – or masks in con-flict. How many challenges do you think might present for the wrong mask chosen for the wrong moment?

Stephanie Paxton is a dear from of mine from the TLC Mastermind. She shared that what she thought was working well for her in business was a "take control" Lyssa archetype. The interesting grey area was that she would have described her-self as "Athena" however she was more authori-tarian than Athena who is associated with calm, collected thoughts as she is a part of the brain of Zeus. Stephanie shared with a small group we were in together, "Working with Loren helped me realize that there is more than one way to negotiate conversations so that I can come from my Athena. From a place where everyone can win." She continued that, "There doesn't have to be a winner or loser. The natural feminine nurtures."

Stephanie came from a challenge that many people in my generation face. She and her sisters were kept out of their family business because their father wanted to "protect" them. As a result, they had zero exposure to the workings of the business. She told our Mastermind, "Unfortunately, in protecting us—he limited us." If the sisters had been sons, it would have been different; but he had girls and he wanted them to be "safe and provided for." When he passed away, the business inevitably fell into the three sisters' laps. They strapped on their father's shoes together and took on the challenge of running their family business for a third generation.

When I asked Stephanie what part of her *identity* was pushed the most. She said it was in the area self-worth that she felt the most growth. Somewhere inside she had the feelings of "you didn't earn this." She had to dig deep – and stop taking for granted the 56 years of life experiences that set her up for success as a business leader.

Success opened up for Stephanie when she found the release. The point where she had to let go of her fears of what she could not see in order to open up the space for what is possible. Part of that "release" was of the "hard-nosed" "boss" with the "winner take all" Lyssa mask.

Remember, masks are not our nature. If you realize you are wearing a mask, stop yourself in your tracks—Get Your Bearings. We are meant to be *wild*, to be intuitive, to be a queen, to be simultaneously soft and fierce, to be multi-faceted... and to *listen* to the voice inside your heart. We are meant to use *all* our gifts, to rise with dignity as the goddesses we truly are and to step into our own powerful (untamed) thunder.

In contrast, your multi-faceted truth requires no effort. It simply is. Truth is truth. Truth resonates. It never waivers, and it's a full, unfiltered expression that continually refuels itself.

Instead, I often see people tend to make life harder, more complicated, and harsher than it actually is. Unlike Stephanie with her Lyssa mask, in the absence of stopping to ask themselves truth-returning questions, most people jump to the worst possible, soul-punishing, self-banishing, and thereby paralyzing conclusions.

No wonder it's so easy to get off track, to lose touch with authenticity, and to end up on the sidewalk of the road named "Truth." I've been there. When I think about any person going through this, it breaks my heart. By letting outside voices, old rules, or your own limiting beliefs dictate your life; what are you missing out on? What parts of yourself are you disallowing? What archetypes have you not owned?

Get Your Bearings, pause, re-evaluate and ask yourself some *identity*-grounding questions. You *must* break this cycle—the quality of your wild and true life *depends* on it.

From here forward, when you find yourself in a whirlwind of masked *identity* (maybe on social media), self-loathing or progressed confusion (like Stephanie did while in the first years of running her father's company with her two sisters)—monitor the conversation happening in your head, and practice asking some new questions.

Am I *Staying True* right now?
Is this perception true?
What else could be true?
What else could this mean?
What resources am I not utilizing?
What is an alternate solution?

How can I move forward?
Is this helping?
What's another more empowering story?
Who else am I?
And if you hear yourself saying any of the following to yourself:
Why I am not like _____?
What's wrong with you?
Why am I such a _____ (fill in the blank of degrading, mean words)?
Why can't I do anything right?
Say, "I need to Get My Bearings." Grab your beautiful self-hands-to-cheeks and literally force your face to look in a different direction.
Ask instead:
What do I need right now?
Who am I *really*? Who else am I? What else am I?
Who am I at my fully wild and divine core?
What is my truth?
What are my gifts (all of them)?
How will I rise with dignity?

How will I reclaim my passions and actually speak the language of my dreams? Life is too short for wasting a single second on anything less. From here, your complete *Badass and Beautiful* life is imminent. You're in control, and no one else gets to define you.

Before you turn forward to the next chapter, I invite you to take some time to Get Your Bearings *right now* by starting with the following questions.

Where are you right now? What's your current path?

When you were young, what did you know was your TRUTH?

Do you remember the first time you "stood up for your truth?"

What did it feel like to finally step into your true self?

Who are you *really*? Let's locate your archetype *identity*. What are the words you use to describe yourself? (We could give you a quiz and tell you who you are, but it's more powerful and *true* for you to define for yourself .) Are you a "Badass Boss Babe, a Marvelous Millionare, a Sex Kitten,

an Aligned Leader Rockstar, a Manifest Maven..."
Who are you?

List what you are so proud of yourself for in your life.

When have you had a time when all was going
your way? What did that feel like?

When have you felt shaken, like you were over-burdened? What did it feel like when it all changed?

Give yourself a few powerful adjectives and adverbs for your feelings. "Bad" could be autrocious, devestated, plunging. "Good" could be free, soul-filled-bliss, accomplished.

Is anything holding you down from finding your truth?

What are the "tools" in your personal tool kit? When you sit at the table, what skills can others count on you for? (Again – pull out the Thesaurus and find the words that truly match your feelings. Words have power.)

What gifts do you see in yourself?

What do other people say they see in you?

What do you want more than anything in life?
What would you regret if you did not ?

What will you be so incredibly bummed if you don't accomplish... ?

What is your life's greatest dream?

And, if you want to *really* integrate your purpose, I will help. This year, I launched my Manifest Your _____ Masterclass, where I personally lead people through the process of creating and attaining their vision. If you'd like to join me, find my next event at lorenlahav.com.

5

RITUALS: CREATE YOUR PATH

Metaphorically speaking, if you were to spin yourself in circles (as life often does), would you be able to pivot to the direction of your true, Badass and Beautiful self? Do you even know the direction you're currently facing? And do you know precisely (or even roughly) where you *want* to go?

Everyone has let their wild woman fall silent and even die at some point in life. In spite of lulls in personal strength or even failures, connecting to your truth is how you will rise like a phoenix back to your chosen path every time. Let me explain.

Life is cyclical. As a result, people gravitate toward patterns. Seasons and stages are a part of this fabric of humanity. Rituals are the punctuation marks in the passing of seasons and of time—they help celebrate and therefore transition people from one stage or opportunity to the next. Rituals can support day-to-day spiritual, mental, physical, and emotional health. They support progression and build community. Ultimately, rituals are foundational as they set a solid boundary for what you will and will not allow to occur in your life.

Just as the sun consistently rises every day, rituals represent new beginnings, awakening and unlimited potential. Contrarily, rituals also bring closure. The process of human growth and evolution is a broad series of moments—like a photographic mosaic. From this perspective, rituals can be several things:

— A way to celebrate life

— A way to show gratitude

— A way to build community and strengthen ties

— A way to goal set

— A way to intentionally create patterns for progress

— A way to wind down

— A way to say good-bye

— A way to end a year in preparation for a new beginning

In fact, any culture that has sustained the test of time has done so because of the rituals stacked behind it. When you think about it, rituals actually connect humans throughout history—beyond space and time. Staggeringly, rituals define core values not only for the individual, but also for the collective.

When anthropologists work to understand an ancient civilization, the rituals practiced consistently by its people become one of the most important ways to analyze their needs, priorities and relationships.

Rituals give people a sense of control. They provide a comforting sense of forward momentum, something we all crave, frankly—because they work. You can hit the gas pedal hard or go light, but over time, the consistency of rituals creates results.

Our most primal instinct is to survive. Small wins from rituals bring serotonin to the body, and over time, the cumulative effect of seemingly ordinary activities can create a long-term sense of well-being, and documented studies from some of the world's most respected, credible sources such as Harvard Business School prove this fact. Routine serotine boosts triggered by seemingly "regular" activities performed consistently leave people feeling happier and more fulfilled. In addition, these results are cumulative—the more the activity is performed, the happier people become.

Even more importantly, historically, rituals have served as the lifeline that saves us even when everything sane, kind and just has vanished. For example, during the Holocaust, Jewish people in the ghettos practiced something called "Spiritual Resistance." The prisoners were able to maintain their humanity, integrity, and dignity by continuing to practice Shiva to honor the deceased and Shabbat. Shabbat is the seventh day of the week which is Friday at sunset to Saturday at sunset in the Jewish calendar. It is a day to remember the story of creation from the Torah and "The Exodus," the freedom of the Jews from slavery in Egypt in 1310 BCE. The day is to be a day of rest. To practice this ritual, candles are lit and blessings are done over bread and wine.

There is a story from the Holocaust of a person who worked in a jacket factory. There was a certain number of jackets that were the day's quota. If the quota was exceeded by one, the prisoner was given extra bread. This survivor made three extra jackets a day and hid them in a discarded pile of remnants. This way, they were able to honor the Sabbat with a day of rest if they "pretended" to work every time the people in charge of the prisoners walked by.

A second Holocaust story is from Auschwitz. Stories have survived of women saving margarine and using threads from their dresses so that they could have Shabbat candles to light on Friday 18-min before sunset.

Together, the prisoners would count the days to Shabbat. The light of the candles signifies "delight and illumination" in this ritual. They are not to be extinguished. Can you imagine the hope and actual illumination this ritual provided for the people in those 44,000 Nazi camps, incarceration sites, and ghettos from 1933-1945?

No matter how the Nazis tried to degrade and dehumanize, it was these rituals that allowed the sense of civilization to root them to survival.

Taking this ritual to the root of lighting the menorah on Hannukah. The meaning behind the season of light is that a lot of light can come from very little oil. Each time the ritual of a candle lit in captivity transpired more than a few prisoners had to of been reminded of this connection shared with the earliest Jews throughout all of time.

But rituals are also a way to bring needed meaning to important life stages and transitions. Modern Aztecs still perform the dance of Xochitl-Quetzal, which translates to "precious flower feather," and is a healing ceremony intended to protect fertility, beauty and love. In Kuala Lumpur, pilgrims celebrate Thaipusam, a Hindu festival honoring gratitude and devotion, by climbing 272 steps up to a cave at midnight. Native Americans are known to celebrate both death and the elderly. They believed old age to be a sign of a life well-lived, and consider death to be the start of life in the Spirit World. As such, tribes honor the dead by giving them food, herbs and gifts to ensure a safe passage to the other side.

In addition, rituals create connection. Intimate couples report finding more meaning and satisfaction in their relationship when they enjoy shared rituals. This is true for not only couples, but for whole communities. Healing Circles or Hocokah—also known as "Peacemaking Circles" are a ritual I admire a great deal from the Native North American cultures.

The circle is symbolic of the Medicine Wheel. (It is also symbolic of the directionals of the traditional Compass Rose.) Because the elderly are revered and honored for their wisdom, the tribes show respect by taking the time to sit with their elders and listen to their wisdom. Members of the tribes sit in a circle and ponder a question with their most elderly members. The elderly members pass a "talking stick" adorned with ornamental objects and feathers. It is passed one to the other and only the person holding the "talking stick" can share (one at a time). During modern times, similar shared circle rituals have been used spiritually, as well as in addiction recovery support programs.

Rituals such as these pass on *truth*: knowledge, values, and culture. They can also break up the mundane or simply celebrate the morning sun.

The Winter Solstice has many different ways to be celebrated throughout the world. The Celts believed that the season of darkness right before the shortest day of the year was a time of reflection and gratitude. They believe "the veil" between the ancestors who had already passed was thinnest during this period of darkness. It was also believed that the lights of the bonfire or the candles in their windows on this night were a way to ward of the darkness. The next day, the morning of December 22 would be a time for great celebration. For they believed the darkness had been won over by the light and that this would mean the entire Earth would survive and thrive a whole new year.

These days before the start of the year equal 12 (hence the song "The 12-days of Christmas") By the 1700s 12-day Christmas celebrations were known as "The Season" and were actually an answer to "Seasonal Depression" (another kind of darkness). Rather than suffering through a long, lonely, cold winter—people celebrated life and the end of the year, traveling to each other's homes for parties. They would stay for four-days at minimum and enjoy dances, meals, and traditions together.

Most intimately, rituals are anchored back to your *identity*. So, when you say that your *identity* is that of a Fit Foxy Vixen (*if you remember from the last chapter, that's mine!),* do your rituals (daily, weekly, monthly and annually) back you up? Have you defined your own daily, weekly, monthly, quarterly, ½ annual, and annual rituals?

What kind of rituals do you think Lee's archetypes have (trust me there are many)?

Or, are you scrambling to get through each day blindly with hope it will get done, without realizing consciously the activities you're consistently choosing?

Ultimately, to create congruent rituals that bring you back to your truth is to create patterns of success. Rituals take dedication, commitment, and intention. To choose your rituals (and live them) is to empower yourself to live your true and fullest life. And when it comes to actually living *your life*—let this soak in—you either *take action* or you *stay stuck*. There are no other options. You can *intend* and *try* all you want. You can plan, and visualize and dream—which is all worthwhile and has it's place, but unless you Get Off Your Ass (GOYA) and actually do something, it is all for not.

If I said to you—*"What will your life look like in five, 10 or 20 years?"* Do you know? Is your vision aligned with the action you are taking to get to that goal? Creating your vision is a ritual in itself. When you combine it with the strength of the *identity* of an archetype, you may be unstoppable.

Vision + Action = Success

In his book, "Think and Grow Rich," Napoleon Hill outlines a letter-writing ritual. The idea is that every morning and night when you are working toward a goal, you read this letter you write to yourself. I took this practice one step further.

At any new chapter or significant milestone in my life, and at least once a year as a reset, I create a Manifestation Board. Manifestation Boards are one of my trademarks. Much like Hill's letter, you start with the end in mind. In your mind, you visualize what your life will be like when your goals in mind are no longer as Louisa May Allcott would have said, "castles in the air" yet have become reality. This is one of my favorites. If you've never done it before, here's how it works...

Grab a stack of magazines you like (start with some good content). Then, with your goals in mind, grab your scissors and cut out photos and words you'd like to draw into your life. Organize and post these pictures—with double-sided tape or glue on a board and place your finished product where you can continually reference the images daily.

Rituals aren't complicated, but they can have a huge impact, individually. They can be a simple habit for grounding yourself. For example, when I go on the road for events and speaking engagements, I set up a picture of my kids on my hotel-room desk. I always take the time to unpack my bags, to organize my stuff and to take a moment to become present with myself in the place where I am staying. This creates a sense of "home" for me and gives my psyche space to feel at peace with my surroundings.

Rituals exist in places you may have over-looked. For instance, the practice of "returning to breath." When I get into a state that will not serve me, I instinctively draw in a centering breath to find clarity. This allows my heart and mind time to connect. Your heart was beating before your brain was working and when you give your heart time to connect to your brain, this is a place for magic.

During our True Voice Intensive, my team and I teach people the power of the "pause." Sometimes, when in front of others, your nerves get the best of you. You can get your bearings by taking a deep breath which allows your heart and mind to connect. From this comes resolve, and clear communication.

I started this practice for myself when I was that 18 year-old Army ROTC candidate sorority girl. During that training exercise with the compass I mentioned earlier, I got lost and had to find my way back with only my map and that real-life compass. There was a moment of fear when I started to panic, but somehow remembering this practice of breath came to me right at that pivotal moment. It saved me.

One simple breath can take you from running away to, "Okay, I got this." Think of the power of taking a moment to send calming hormones throughout your body and allow your nerves to realize, "I've got this!"

That's the power of rituals. It's a simple way to participate in your own rescue—over and over again. But they don't start out that way.

They can be scrappy and inconsistent to start, requiring effort, internal reminders, forgiveness over failures or deviations and constant mindfulness. But let's be clear—it's more than worth it.

Chances are you have many "rituals in place." This is where I ask you: "Do your rituals support your life?"

With more and more people working from home, the ability to create and maintain rituals for yourself is increasingly important. Do you wake up in the morning, get straight on email without leaving your bed, never change out of your pajamas (or maybe just change your top – "business on the top, party on the bottom" for a Zoom call)? Do you never leave the computer (or feel massive guilt if you do)? Do you stay up late and repeat the entire process all over again?

I just called my friend on this. This behavior is not her—she is a ritual-focused momma, who runs her home on balance from boundaries, but she's in a place where she feels she needs the certainty and security from going the extra mile at work, and her balance is off.

Recently, the seasonal "bug" took her completely "out-of-commission" for a much longer time than if she had been holding space for the practices she needs to stay healthy. She had been looking forward to attending the MyVegas luncheon and our Stay True Creative Production launch in Las Vegas, but found herself at home in bed. This is the consequence of not honoring your rituals. Imbalance leads to lack of wellness. When people do not take this time for themselves, their bodies eventually "over-ride" and begin to call the shots.

My friend needs to re-establishing rituals that serve her success, rather than continuing with her current rituals that have removed all boundaries. Since she works from home, it is important that she re-introduces the boundary of "work" space and "home" space. This will allow her to more fully recharge when "off-the-clock" and gives herself the "permission" to feel "un-plugged" from being "on" all the time. She needs to work her healthy routine rituals back into the time blocks of her day. Her children need face-to-face time with their mom to be included in those time blocks. The other day I asked, "What's one thing you can do to start back to where you want to be?" She mentioned green drink. I suggested a really great wheat grass.

When your rituals align and therefore reinforce the direction you want to be going in life, it is a matter of time before you are simply in a pattern for success. Then, if you find yourself all spun around and off-course, *any* one of your rituals can pull you back and put you on track. Like cogs in a machine, one ritual brings you back to your truth. From there, you find another and latch on to it. And then another. Until you are in-synch with your true path again.

The exponential impact is more than you think it will be and sort of a miracle-in-the-making, in retrospect.

A few years ago, I wrote a book called *Life Tune-Ups*. The concept of this book is that rituals are the fuel for life. It's stocked full of my favorite, simple life hacks and best practices, the ones that have given me an unparalleled return on investment. As this book reveals, you don't actually need a whole new career, a whole new relationship, or a whole make-over to create your badass and beautiful life. You don't have to give up everything and start all over; it's the little shifts that matter.

When you set the intended speed on your cruise control and decide you want to speed up or slow down you have two choices. First, you can press the button to turn off the cruise control, put your foot on the gas or press the brake, and then set the new intended speed. The second option, simply press the arrow key on the steering wheel with your finger up or down a few mph.

In this way, you can influence the course you're on by defining and then adjusting the *small nuances* that matter to you. And in doing so, you become able to do more than most people even dream of.

Take a moment now to consider the rituals in your life. What do you do consistently, every day?

Do all of your rituals support your life? Are there any rituals you may need to eliminate?

And have you been trying to manually course correct a ritual (swinging back and forth from going so hard you burn yourself out or not doing it all) when you only needed to "trim out your course" by making a minor personalized adjustment?

To help get your wheels turning, here is a list of some of my favorite rituals:

— Spinning in circles in the woods

— Taking a bath to recharge

— Journaling

— Creating Vision Boards

— Sponsoring Monthly Birthday Parties at the Title 1 School in Las Vegas

— Creating Manifesting Boards

— Thanksgiving Meals I provide every year for families who would have none

— Calling my mom every day (Special note: Life is precious and I am lucky to still be able to do this last one. My oldest son, Jos, noticed this practice and asked me about it. Acknowledging how special it is to connect daily with those you love most in gratitude for their role in your life. He now takes the time to daily call both me and his dad.)

Are there rituals you recognize as having "made all the difference" so far in your life?

For me, the most important ritual of all is physically taking care of my body. The foundational level of all-life is wellness. If you do not have your health, you have nothing. A decade ago, I came into line with an amazing company that's fruits and vegetables in a capsule. Here I was, the "Green Drink" girl—running around Fiji and all over the world teaching people how important it is to support their personal shifts beginning with nutrition. Then, I learned of a company that makes eating organic, whole, non-GMO fruits and vegetables even more accessible and actionable, anywhere in the world.

Every morning, I still drink my green juice and play my favorite song, I call it my anthem. The song changes (when I was going through my divorce, it was *Wide Open Spaces* by the Chicks, now—it is usually Pink), but the practice is the same.

What are your anthems? What are songs that will bring you to a place of peace, power, or pure joy?

Rituals are small, but mighty little promises to yourself. At the time we take them on, they seem small and relatively unimportant. Like a ring-tone that brings a smile. The sum of all the parts is they compound to make all the difference. Reinforcing your Badass and Beautiful *identity* and bringing her back to "home" while you take action to achieve your masterpiece mosaic vision—your life.

As you define and refine your own rituals—a word of caution. In a weirdly self-sabotaging way, rituals, when not grounded in *your truth*, can be a trap. Just as in every part of living your badass and beautiful life, you can't adopt someone else's rituals and successfully apply them blindly to your own life. Nor can you dictate your own rituals with rigidity. It's a balance that only you can manage and define.

Just as if you were holding a palmful of sand, if you squeeze too tight, the sand falls through the cracks. The key to life-changing rituals is to hold your practices softly with awareness. There is a time to push yourself, but there is also a time to dance with the day and to allow it all to unfold without restriction.

This is again—a paradox, requiring both a method and genius. The method is to define the rituals that will take you from where you are now to where you want to go. The genius is to become a creative director in your own life and redefine the rituals in the moment to fit the parameters of the day because life can be unexpected.

And in fact, the genius is often a practice of discipline greater than the method—you have to know what you can control, and what you can't (or shouldn't). As a mother, I know I've had plenty of days when I planned my day with the best intentions to follow through with rituals such as getting my workout in or studying a foreign language, and then... someone forgot their lunch... and I have to drive across town unexpectedly to deliver it. The same day, there is a huge traffic jam, and then the computer breaks down. Kids, technology, traffic, work; these can all derail plans quickly. It's not an easy balance to strike, but the goal is to allow space for both grace and spontaneity.

Ironically, *Staying True* can also mean knowing when it's best to simply sit on your bum and ignore all rituals. Some people can get up at 4 am and feel energized all day. If I did that, I would be holding my eyes open with toothpicks and not giving my best, to anything. Free divers who practice holding their breath to go deeper, and then deeper into the ocean—no thank you, not part of my path and therefore not a practice I need to take on.

My husband, Z, and I have a ritual we call "six o'clock and we're done." This means no phone calls, no last-minute emails or projects. Once six o'clock rolls around, it is our time to be together and fully present. (PS—I may or may not have snuck my phone into the bedroom at 10 pm at night to get these final edits complete.)

Here's the bottom line: Rituals only work if they align with your deepest truth and *identity*. You must listen closely to hear the whisper of your own soul. You have to know who you are and what makes *you* feel most alive before you can define them.

I can't tell you what rituals to take on, or even where to start, no one can. Knowing who you are and what you need—that's staying true. There's an inner voice, an inner compass inside you, that *knows*. But you have to slow down to hear it and respect the advice from your own heart once you hear it. Are you listening? Will you?

You have to understand your desired outcome first. Then, "get resourceful." Rather than beating yourself up, becoming a mean self-dictator, simply point yourself in the right direction and make being kind to yourself the highest priority ritual.

Defining just one key "lifeline" ritual is often all that it takes. What that might look like, for example, if your planned ritual is a daily yoga practice—can you give yourself a golden star for five minutes in child's pose? There is not a singular recipe to success—you must write your own. Only you know if you "cheated" or skipped a day.

First, step away and unpack the noise. That's the real obstacle. As we've already established, we are literally exposed to billions of bits of information every day. An art in itself is to ignore those things that don't actually serve. It gets easier the more you practice it.

Here are some suggestions for you to try:

— Take a walk in nature.

— Create a "sacred space" in your home.

— Take a bath with candles completely surrounding you.

— Turn on some music and dance like a truly Badass and Beautiful Woman.

I don't care where you've been. Every day, every moment is new. And at this very moment, you can choose a new path. *Seize this moment and begin.*

I've crafted some questions to help you create a roadmap from here. Before moving on to the next chapter, take some time to give these questions some thought. Then reach inside your own heart. Strike a deal with yourself that you promise and pinky-swear you will follow-through. Just make sure your answers are realistic so that you can keep the promise and honor the commitment.

Here we go.

What are the rituals in your life right now?

What is 1 new small ritual you will begin, starting tomorrow, to reinforce your truth?

What is the trajectory of this, played out over the next 5 years? 10 years?

What is 1 big action you will take, sometime this month, to reinforce your truth?

What is a ritual you have always meant to practice and never followed through with?

What is one action you can take right now to include this in your life? Grab your calendar and block the time right now.

What is a ritual that is no longer serving you? How can you eliminate it?

What are rituals you have observed in others that you respect? What do these rituals mean to you? How would your life improve to include these in your life?

Think of successful people you admire in the world or even your favorite archetypes. Do a little research to find out what their rituals are. Are these rituals you should include in your own life?

STEP 2:
OWN IT!

6
BOUNDARIES: THE QUEEN'S CHAMBERS

Let's be honest—boundaries are an artform that takes time to master. Even then, you may have to redefine after time. "Boundaries?" you say. "Loren is all over the place!"

At first glance, I may seem like a hurricane, but behind the scenes—I love my planner, I like everything to be labeled, I set up a schedule for the entire year (every year), I create time blocks for work and make master spreadsheets. I carry a label maker with me at all times. Yep, it's true.

Over the years, I've been getting better at it all—not because I'm getting even more structured, but because I've realized that there is a finite correlation between structure (or boundaries) and abolishing the trap of being an over-pleaser. *I'm sure none of you can relate to this?* (Ha!-Ha!)

This is the number one key to *OWN IT!*

So many of us are rooted in this pattern of *pleasing to the point of martyrdom*. Pleasing others at this level is the opposite of healthy boundaries. Here is yet another wakeup call.

Let me explain.

One of my deepest desires for you (and every woman I meet) is to step into your sovereignty. The sovereign is the Queen archetype. Everyone deserves to be a Queen in their own right. That's why I titled my flagship event, *Own Your Worth*. I want you to *know* and celebrate how amazing you are, how much you have to give, how beautiful and how special you are. I *believe* that you are a badass and beautiful queen. When you think of a queen what do you think of? What does a queen represent? She represents OWNING IT. The female ruler of her country. The queen is elegance, leadership, confidence, and strength. The spiritual meaning of a queen is the divine feminine that allows a woman to present her highest and best version of herself to the world. Why wouldn't you step into your queen? It is time to call out the queen. Does she queen scare you?

Tracie Munce is one of my head Trainers. She owns Merlin's Rest and Eagan Arms Public House. Her events are Women's Entrepreneur Happy Hour and Women's Power Luncheons. Last winter, her meat pies were the ones Burberry sold for the holiday season. Her book is The EAPH Factor: Hospitality for Everyday. I asked her to share with me her sovereign queen experience.

What immediately came to mind for Tracie was one of the stories that deeply impacted her during our TLC trip to the Dominican Republic hosted by a dear friend of mine, Lucy. Someone asked Lucy how she handles chaotic situations. Lucy explained that when she enters a room filled with chaos, she emotionally places her back against the wall, observing the situation to determine whether her involvement is necessary. If she doesn't feel she can add value, she quietly leaves. This taught Tracie the importance of knowing when to engage and when to step back—a lesson in setting clear boundaries.

Another moment that stood out for Tracie was when she jokingly asked Lucy to show her "pageant walk." Lucy, with the effortless grace of a queen, instantly stood tall, head held high, shoulders back, and moved with a sense of ease and flow. This became a powerful visual and reminder for Tracie to walk through life with confidence, embracing her own power and sovereignty as a leader. These moments of being in Lucy's presence, whether in the labyrinth discussing ancestral wisdom or just watching her interact with others, have deeply shaped Tracie's understanding of self-worth and leadership.

Through her interactions with Lucy, Tracie has learned not just how to set boundaries, but how to embody them with poise, reminding herself that she, too, holds the power to lead and live authentically.

The effects of this have rippled through Tracie's life. This experience with Lucy has profoundly influenced the way Tracie leads, especially in her approach to fostering self-assurance. As a result, the women she leads have stepped fully into their roles with confidence and calm. One of her distinctions is that true leadership doesn't require force or convincing—it's about showing up authentically.

When chaos arises, either with her team or within the day-to-day pressures of running her businesses, Tracie now remembers Lucy's method of standing back to observe before deciding whether to engage. This has allowed her to maintain composure and clarity, ensuring that her involvement is purposeful and impactful rather than reactionary. Tracie has also adopted Lucy's posture of walking with her head held high and shoulders back, which helps her embody a sense of peace and control, even during challenging situations.

Tracie has noticed that when she leads from the heart and stands firm in her own truth, her employees naturally gravitate toward her, respecting and trusting her leadership without her needing to push or pull. Her reverence for her staff, combined with the boundaries she now sets with intention, has fostered a culture of mutual respect and empowerment. It's not just about managing tasks anymore—it's about creating an environment where everyone feels seen, valued, and inspired to bring their best selves to the workplace.

Someone like Lucy and Tracie who fully embraces the archetype of the **Sovereign Queen** is one who holds herself with both dignity and grace, yet her most powerful attribute is her ability to create and maintain boundaries. For her, boundaries are not walls but sacred spaces—like the chambers of her palace—where she reigns with authority and self-respect. These boundaries define what she allows into her life, how she spends her energy, and the quality of her relationships.

She knows that saying "no" is not a weakness but a form of self-love, ensuring that her time and presence are respected. Whether it's in her personal life or her role as a leader, she engages only with situations and people who bring value, joy, and alignment with her purpose. Just as a queen knows who is allowed within the castle walls, this woman knows when to step back from chaos or conflict, only engaging when she feels her presence will add value.

In moments of doubt or challenge, the Sovereign Queen doesn't need to prove herself or seek approval from others. She walks with a regal air, confident in her ability to handle whatever comes her way because she trusts herself fully.

This woman inspires others simply by being in her presence—her calm confidence radiates, lifting those around her. She has learned that her power lies not in controlling others but in mastering herself. Through the art of boundaries, she has created a life of peace, fulfillment, and true sovereignty.

No matter what your past experience, no matter the boundaries you are have or have had crossed. I am with you. More than anything, no matter what, I just want you to wake up and to reclaim your space. Set the framework for the foundation that is your space in this world. Claim it.

No one can take away your grace, beauty, worth, and gifts. Unless you give it to them. This is not an option.

It's time to take it back.

A few years ago, I interviewed Kaylin Marcotte, creator of Jiggy Puzzles, on my Podcast, *Stay True*. She makes puzzles for a living. She's been featured on Shark Tank, in *Forbes*, on *CNN,* and inside *Elle* magazine, among many others. I bring her on stage regularly at my *Own Your Worth* events.

Her puzzles have become exceptionally popular because she's taken an innovative approach to this long-lost pastime. By featuring current artwork (from both known and up-and-coming, not-yet-discovered artists), Kaylin makes her puzzle partnerships a win-win-win for her business, the artists she features, and her puzzle-maker patrons. Puzzles, in fact, can represent many beautiful metaphors for life—taking one small step at a time, trying sh** out, getting out of the forest to see the trees, keeping the ultimate vision in mind at all times.

However, the real genius of her creation was in noticing and designing puzzle-making as a way to soothe her own soul. It all began after long days launching a start-up news publication, *The Skimm*. Puzzles soon became her nightly meditation ritual; she used them to wind down. In the process, she began to notice how the practice was informing and integrating her approach to life.

After trying some of Kaylin's puzzles myself, I realized what I absolutely love most about making puzzles, is the pure satisfaction found in starting with the border.

Think about it. No one starts in the middle—that's madness. It's too much trial and error, too many options and a pile of so many overwhelming possibilities. Most of us would give up before even starting. Yes—the simple (almost unanimously shared) process of starting a puzzle is with the border. Here are two core life hacks from puzzle building—(1) start with what you know, and (2) *life is easier once you have some boundaries.*

To further the metaphor and to love on Kaylin even more—I also appreciate her vision to show-case the work of artists. In fact, her puzzles are so pretty, many people actually frame them as "forever art" in their homes. (Which was actually also a part of her original, beautiful, and brilliant business design.) This concept extends the meta-phor—if you give yourself clear boundaries in life, you have the freedom to design your own mas-terpiece within that framework. How beautiful is that?

It sounds straightforward and easy. However, although almost everyone starts with the borders when making a puzzle, almost *no one* does so in real life.

So, why do we settle?

It's simple, just like in the instance of social media from a previous chapter—we want everyone to love us, or even more so, not to *unlove* (or unfol-low) us. Most of us get through life, churning away, trying to make ends meet while pleas-ing everyone else. We don't slow down enough to gain perspective. For whatever reason, be it self-preservation or some other extraneous cause, we find ourselves jumping from one conclusion to another. When the solution may be as simple as, *"What do I really want?"*

A few months ago, I spent some quality time going through the reviews from *Own Your Worth*. With each review, I noted a common theme among the participants—the highlight for so many people was a newfound ability to *forgive themselves* of failures—both perceived and imagined. Dreams that were let go, people that were let down, commitments that didn't pan out, promises that were broken. Whether real or imagined, self-forgiveness was needed for unaccomplished goals.

I could see the absolute truth and beauty of each of these women. Why on Earth would they all think they needed to be forgiven? I was surprised with the sheer volume of people placing themselves in the line of people seeking redemption in order to progress in life. What was going on, I wondered. Why is this such a central theme? A sign of our times? Why?

I read a blog back in 2019 that found that self-criticism is part of evolution. In conclusion, the blog suggested for emotional-wellness we practice the "Golden Rule," "Do unto others as you would have them do unto you..." on ourselves.

Another observation I would see over and over (again), this theme of being *tired*. Why are women everywhere so *tired*? The reason, I think, is a conflicting desire to play so many different roles (or too much of the same) to please others—a lack of boundaries.

When building a puzzle, have you ever sat with a table-full of shapes and sizes all of uncharacterizable similar color? Just as puzzles contain multiple pieces that seem meaningless without the structure of the border to work from, humans also contain a vastness. Rather than contain and focus that energy, most of us unconsciously let it spill out in all directions.

In many ways we take the energy, our lifeforce, for granted. We expect our bodies to just keep giving, without filling ourselves back up—often without even the basic essential nutrients (healthy meals, quality sleep, genuine connection) required to survive. Ironically, in this dance, we're all trying to make each other *happy*.

A friend told me a story recently about a guest who was in town visiting. Both the guest and the host had planned to do dinner upon the guest's arrival. However, when she arrived, my friend had had an unexpectedly rough week and was exhausted. The idea of going out was not a healing recipe, but he didn't want to let the visitor down. In a sort of f***-it moment, rather than just going to please the guest, he decided to be fully honest and said, "I'm actually pretty tired and don't want to go out, but if you want to, I will absolutely go with you."

To his surprise, the guest responded, "Ah, I'm actually really tired too. Likewise, I didn't want to let you down."

How often do we do this "for" each other? Thinking we are being "kind and supportive" we please one another. The result? Nobody honestly expresses their truth. In the end, everyone is walking around making concessions without having their actual needs met. Eventually, all involved walk away empty.

Boundaries (i.e. the borders that protect leaky energy) essentially come down to communication—*really, really clear* communication. To act without knowing *exactly* the needs of ourselves and others often results in a very pointless charade. It's all so beautiful and ridiculous at the same time.

Meanwhile, internally, many of us keep score. "Well, I went to that special dinner with you even when I was exhausted (not that I told you that), but now I need someone to help me, and you're not there?" Trees in the forest do not keep score. They grow, add to the community, and hold no grudges – we probably would be better at our job of being our best version of ourselves if we did not either.

Ever hear of the Irish Exit? I'm famous for this trick. When it gets to the point that I'm over-tired in a group of people, sometimes it is all I can do to socialize and "fake it." It is as if my body has a built-in boundary (of a bedtime). So, when it is "time" for me to go – I simply slip out the back-door. People will turn and say, "Where did Loren go?" And I am half-way to my bathtub and bed! When kids are little—this is one of the first places they learn about boundaries, the bedtime. There are entire shelves of books about how to transition your kids to a successful night-time ritual. The Irish Exit or a bedtime are actually a physiological boundary. If I were not to "slip out the backdoor" and honor my need for sleep, I could end up sick.

When you get down to it boundaries are really about clarity, truth and tough conversations. Boundaries mean that "no" is a honest "no," and then that "yes" is truly a "yes" (not just a "yes" because I *think* it's what you want). Without this level of honesty, a fake "yes" is just a few exchanges away from *bitter*—the sort of internal acid that eats away at your soul. In this way, a fake "yes" (i.e. a lack of boundaries) ends up hurting both you *and* the person you care about.

We all want to love and to be loved. We want to support and be there for the people we care about. However, if we don't clearly express the needs and desires of our true inner archetype *badass and beautiful woman*—no matter how strange we think her voice may sound to others, no one actually ends up happy. A "NO" is a normal and natural response; no one wants everything all the time. This is why building a solid structure or framework around your needs is an essential art; yet one that we're often too polite to practice.

In hindsight this is what happened in my marriage. We were both trying *really* hard to please one another, but since we didn't communicate, we were both "*doing things*" for each other that neither of us really wanted. Sadly, this paradigm is pretty common.

While I was going through my divorce, I was deep in a sort of "hunker down" state. I was in the middle of trying to figure out my finances. How was I going to survive? How was I going to provide for my kids' needs? In the process of self-survival mode, I'd pretty much cut myself off from all my friends and all social events. It was what I needed to get myself through the chaos.

And then my phone rang. I could see that it was one of my very dear friends. I knew that she was probably calling with a request of some kind because I am known by my friends as the type of person who loves to connect people with solutions. However, in this moment, I didn't have the resources on every level—including time.

I was weighing the options in my mind while the phone was ringing. And then suddenly, it struck me, I can just tell her what is actually going on. I don't have to be the "regular" me. What if I just tell her upfront, "This is what's going on. I only have 10 minutes. Connecting with you is important to me. Even if just for a moment, we can lift each other up and make a point to call each other when we have more time."

So that's what happened. And that's all the framework I needed to set. She made me laugh, I made her laugh, and we reminded each other of the love in our lives. It was exactly the fuel we both needed to keep going. But we ended the call in just 10 minutes (I set a timer to keep us honest).

This truth works in tandem with your *identity*. When you are clear about who you are, you can then reinforce that with what you will and will not stand for. If our words and actions reflect the truth of our thoughts—solid boundaries are automatic. Other people know who you are, what you stand for, and can be certain that when you interact with them, they can trust you.

Ironically, boundaries in real-life are a framework. Think fences, picture frames, boxes, borders, walls; but in human relationships—a boundary is full transparency of wants, needs, philosophies, and limits.

With all of this, a boundary isn't a "maybe." A boundary is human's unique ability to carve out the actual space where we can best grow as individuals, thus expanding into the best versions of ourselves. As this happens, we are empowered to contribute our greatest gifts to that whole—honoring our worth and ensuring we have more to give in the long-run.

Because of this, a boundary must be done with congruency and solidarity. You can draw a line and share it with someone else; but, until you give that line the energy of conviction, it's like trying to hold water with a wall of sponges.

Think of a boundary as a "soul contract" with yourself and others. When you are in business, a contract establishes the conditions you agree to work under. The times you will share your energy. The amount of money you are willing to accept for the life-force you put into a project. You may require benefits, vacation, flex-hours, child-care, or lattés. If someone does not pay you on time or refuses to supply you with something you both agreed to within the contract, the relationship suffers—and perhaps ends. I always say, "You never hear of a relationship breaking up because people communicated too much."

There are many common reasons to make common contracts—you have a contract to get married, to start a child in a new academic program, to bring your dog into a pet-friendly hotel—we have contracts with all kinds of people and entities, but it dawned on me—we don't establish a contract with ourselves.

Instead, we seem to be "pleasing" machines. We shift our energy from one immediate need and direction to the next. We ask ourselves questions;

but, the inquiries are: What will make our significant other happy? What makes our children happy? How can we make the boss happy? Our clients? Our co-workers? Our friends? Our extended family—sisters, brothers, aunts, uncles, second-cousins...? You get the idea.

No wonder everyone is so tired.

Many times, if we do not own our own worth and maintain a clean and tidy boundary—we end up having to apologize. A hard example of this I have is a couple of two really-well matched, lovely people. They had given their all in 20-years of marriage, but through time the wife had allowed her own boundaries to erode. When this happened, she did not "show up" as herself. She was hiding, not only for her husband—but to friends and relatives. Because her boundaries were not firm and her "absolutes" mailable, when un-healthy behaviors creeped into the relationship it wasn't a trickle, but more like someone smashing the entire dam.

Ultimately, through those years, she was not the congruent example to her children that she wanted to be of what a healthy relationship can be; which, took a great deal of dedicated work with a team of professionals to repair.

She shared with me that when she did not "show up as her true self," people started to slowly fade from her life. Friends, relatives, and eventually— her marriage broke down because she was not her true self.

Like the child's song "This Little Light of Mine" warns us not to do, she hid herself. As a result, two beautiful people with nothing but love for one another ended up in a truly ugly and lonely cycle.

In the end, she tearfully apologized to her husband, "If I had maintained my boundaries—I do not know where we would be; but, we would not be where we are right now."

There are some relationships where boundaries become imperative. When addiction and abuse are involved, boundaries are typically the first step toward healing.

In a healthy relationship, boundaries are respected. In a toxic relationship one person chips at or ignores the "fence" of the other. To borrow our puzzle analogy once more, I have observed that in stories of people over-coming addiction and abuse, the turning point for that person was when the combined pieces were once again re-assembled back into a border of their "defined" framework or boundaries.

Sometimes this is a pretty big boundary that leads to legal actions to secure people's boundaries.

The thing to know here is that people are not perfect. We are all a beautiful work in progress. A friend of mine who used to be in local government always says, "If the sign is on the road, there is probably a story behind it." These legal actions might be big and scary, but they exist because sometimes it is what is necessary to establish boundaries and re-establish healthy relationships for people.

The thing to know is that in life, if we pray for patience, G-d will give us experiences that bring patience. If we pray for courage, G-d gives us experiences that teach us courage. If we pray for happy families, sometimes we get the experience we didn't know we needed – to build boundaries so that the collective futures of all of those involved in the family will ultimately be brighter, bigger, better, and more filled with love than ever-imagined.

In the case of my friend, their family had years of trauma and chaos. There were significant spiritual-level wounds to heal from for all four. They let me know that after all was said and done, the family recently experienced a very happy Thanksgiving meal together – on the other side of divorce.

Four people with newly established boundaries, smiling over their meal was the greatest promise for a future-forward-focused life to come. Their friendship re-growing in a significantly healthier emotional state as they partner as parents. Life has found balance.

For those of us committed to helping others (that would be all of us—remember our common *oso-tua* wiring), the hardest sort of boundary is knowing what is not ours to fix.

A friend I've made along the way is a woman named Lois. She was one of the few survivors from a fatal plane crash. Based on this experience, Lois shared a philosophy with me about who she believes succeeds in life. To help me understand, she said to me, "Imagine you are on a crashing plane with 12 other people, but as the plane nose-dives into the water and you get your bearings, you quickly realize that only three people on the plane can swim."

"Once you hit the water and miraculously find yourself gasping for air as you bob in the ocean, you see that most of the people around you are drowning."

"Instinctively, you want to help. Who do you swim toward to save?"

I had no idea how to answer. I simply said, "I think I would want to help everyone and move toward the person closest to me."

'If you are ever in this situation," she replied, "I hope you will swim toward the people with their hands up."

"Why?" I asked. "Don't you want to help the people who need it most?"

She replied, "You would hope so, and that's what I tried to do when we crashed. However, I discovered quickly that when you try to help a drowning person, they actually pull you down with them."

"In the struggle of trying to save someone who was sinking, I had to eventually let go. In the process, I passed up someone else with their hands up—someone asking to be a part of his or her own rescue. That was the only person I was able to save."

Of all the people I've met and stories I've heard throughout my life, this one has always stuck with me. It's a deep lesson for me because I always fight for the underdog, and I definitely have "pleaser" tendencies. Although I will keep up that fight, I've realized that I can't save everyone. I've also realized that a person who doesn't want to invest in their own success is a boundary for me. Ultimately, we are all stewards of our own journey. I can only wake up those who are listening and who are ready to receive their own truth.

How many of you have wanted something so bad for someone else? You don't know why they don't "get it." Their dissent is strong like a wall. You can see what would be helpful and they just keep turning it down. A friend of mine, Wendy, would say, "Oh Loren, that self-help stuff works for you, but that's your thing." I invited her to join me at different events and programs for years. One day, I got the call, "Are you sitting down?" Finally! She had won a ticket to an event. Of course, it has made all the difference; but, she had to be the one to decide.

The greatest gift you can give another person is simply to know and speak your truth in a way that maintains boundaries around your needs and wants—and ultimately your happiness. Basically, it is your *duty* to others to "own your own worth," to be the badass and beautiful *QUEEN* that you are! She is waiting. Wake that girl up!

In order to do this, you will first have to listen (deeply) to yourself.

What do you *really* love?

What makes you *feel fully* loved?

If you could make all the noise and all the opinions go dark, what does *your* heart desire? What needs do you need account for to make this happen?

When your mind wanders – where does it go? (Most likely, this is the desire of your heart.) What do you need to do to be sure this space is protected for it to bloom and grow?

What are your "musts?"

How will you allow others to treat you? What is okay with you? What is a "no-go?"

What are your non-negotiable deal-breakers? What will you not allow into your life?

Don't know how to answer these questions. I do. You might find some of these answers now you might find some later. This is a guidebook for you to come back to along the way.

The second, and most easy parameter to establish: Time. There are 10,080 minutes in a week. That seems like plenty, but put in this perspective, most of us only have 80-90 summers in a lifetime.

Yesterday, a loved one was told he doesn't have long to live. A 91-year-old, retired General. With friends all over the world, five grandchildren, and three kids. Someone who found love twice and he loves G-d his whole life.

The kind of human people turn to for wisdom and advice, whether on matters of state at Congressional hearings or on something practical as building construction. A respected leader in his community, he's known for his fairness and optimistic outlook on life. Retired in a beautiful home on the water in North Carolina, where he has spent the last two decades enjoying life surrounded by the love of his friends and family.

His doctor let him know there is not much more they can do for him—his heart is failing. The doctor said, "Look, the average life expectancy is 78, you got 13 years on them! How many people from the class of 1933 are still alive?" Though his body is weakening, his mind is sharp. A reminder time is finite, no matter how well-lived, we always want more.

This truth often hides in plain sight. Days pass by, routines fall into place, and time slips away. Yet, deciding how you choose to spend the time you have each day is one of the most import-ant choices you'll ever make. If you're not clear about what you will and won't dedicate your time to, what can you truly be clear about? To begin...

Set time blocks. Set times in your calendar for the things that fill you up — family, self-care, wellness, reading, learning, dance, celebration, exploring... Live life fully.

One way I set time blocks is to create a "Take 5." This is both a boundary for time and a ritual. Everyone knows I set my alarms for my "Take 5." The outcome is to take just 20 minutes to fill your cup in *all* major areas of life.

For me, I take five minutes for my spirit. I take five minutes for calling. 5 minutes of exercise, plus 5 minutes of journaling, 5 minutes of hugging (perhaps just yourself), 5 minutes of gratitude, 5 minutes of self-care (hello salt scrub!), and 5 minutes of fresh creative idea brainstorming.

Here's another approach: create a system to gauge your emotions. Just like the warning lights on your car's dashboard, this will help you detect when something needs attention. As you go through your day, take note of what activities are draining your energy and which ones are fueling you. Identify the emotion or feeling each activity triggers and assign it a score. This will help you stay aware of your emotional state and take action where needed.

Then we go back to rituals. What rituals will you establish in your life to honor your boundaries? One simple, key example for me—bath time. This is one of my favorite boundaries. And yes, I have a whole tub full of ducks (and you should too!). It is a space where I can wash off the negative residue from the day, go silent, meditate and then come back to life refueled.

If you'd like more examples (including a sample contract for you to use), I'm happy to share! Go to lorenlahav.com – in fact, share your own while you are there!

7

THE SHOES MATTER

There is an old metaphor about the train of life. The train is in constant motion. In fact, it's moving so fast, there's no real time to appreciate (or even fully see) the scenery out the windows. It's spinning along, moving forward—quickly advancing to each "next" destination.

The train does make several stops. And in fact, everyone on-board keeps saying they will get off the train to enjoy the views once they get to the "next" stop—after the graduation, after the wedding, after the project, after the divorce, and on and on... But very few passengers ever actually step off the train.

Meanwhile, the true beauty of life keeps passing by—always present, albeit blurry through the windows.

Even on the inside of the train, most people are staring straight ahead, keeping to themselves. They could be sitting right next a soulmate, a potential new client, a connection maven with helpful needed resources or perhaps even a living angel embodied in human form. But everyone is too busy in their own mind, caught up with their own story, worries and fears to appreciate what's already there.

Serendipity and divine intervention is available... if we are awake enough to receive it. In this way, simply being *awake* is synonymous with *deep gratitude*.

You can't *Own Your Worth, Your Truth, Your Mission, Your Purpose, Your Voice* - if you're not appreciating the opportunities already at your fingertips.

For instance—I met my husband in baggage claim.

When I went through my divorce everybody left. My Mom moved back to the East coast, my ex back to Oregon, my best friend back to California—and it was just me and my kids in Las Vegas. I felt so alone. I didn't have anybody who could watch my kids or help me if I needed support. I woke up in the morning and fell asleep at night thinking, "What do I do?"

The idea came to me, "*What if I move back to CA? At least I'll have friends. I won't be so alone.*"

I took the last bit of money I didn't have to put a down rent deposit on a house in Encinitas. First month's rent, last month's rent, and a security deposit all paid on my credit card. I had made a decision. She was counting on me.

In California, I could take the kids out of private school and put them in really good public schools. Instead of classes and extracurricular activities, they could go to the beach and surf.

Plan in motion. I would fly to Fiji to facilitate a program and when I returned, I would move us back to California.

At the poles we tell everybody the first 10-feet is about leaving your baggage behind. I was out there all day coaching the participants, "Leave your baggage behind!"

Then, the universe took me way too seriously. On my way to Italy for another event, my baggage was left behind.

Luggage lost, I arrived in Italy with the clothes on my back and I kid you not—not one person offered for me to have a change of clothes the entire event.

Like I said, this was right after our divorce and I needed every dime to pay for the sitters while I was out of the country. Buying clothes to wear while I waited for my bags to arrive was out of the question financially.

After the event, in the same clothing I had been in for days, I felt like the clothing on my body could stand up on its own. I was as much the black jeans and cowboy boots as they were me.

Every day I had hoped I would receive even my toiletry bag, but never did they come. Now, I'm grateful I lost my luggage and at the time it felt like a total disaster.

What exactly was in those bags? For Fiji, I had taken all of my best summer clothes. For Italy,

I had taken all of my best Winter clothes. With these bags gone, it felt like everything I needed to keep my life together was suddenly gone. I truly had nothing. The truest sense of losing it all.

By day 8, I was one day away from full reimbursement for my lost baggage. Yet, even this was contentious, because I took different airlines and both airlines were blaming the other. It felt like I was in all over divorce again.

I was petrified. Every part of me wanted to hang on. Every part. I finally decided it was time to surrender, "I just have to let it go."

The gift in losing my luggage, was in the beauty of surrendering attachment (forced though the lesson was).

Do you need to take inventory? Is there some baggage you need to lose?

Finally free from where I had been stuck, slate clean, I went shoe shopping.

Who did I need to be for my family? I needed to be the Queen. What shoes would remind me to stand tall like a proud sovereign?

Black, platform sandals, of course.

There, in Italy, I bought my "first" new pair of shoes. Who doesn't want Italian, platform, black leather to be the first pair of shoes of your "new me?"

I still wear these sandals 13 years later. When I put them on, I am very intentional. If I am going through a tough time and questioning whether or not I can do something, I put them on as a reminder that I already got through the hard times. They remind me of the future *identity* I was claiming that is now reality. That moment when I said, "I got this! I'll figure it out." And it really did happen.

The shoes matter. I know I access different parts of myself each time I reach for a pair. When you see me walk on stage or at an event in town, you can be certain my shoe choice is not just some random pair thrown on before heading out the door.

My shoes are a metaphor for how I walk through life. What about you?

Are you stumbling around in something that doesn't fit? Are your shoes painfully holding you back? Are you laced up in something that makes you feel unstoppable?

Just like the right pair of shoes can make you stand taller, move faster, or dance a little longer, the choices you make every day must propel you forward.

So, ask yourself: are you wearing the shoes that'll get you to where you want to go, or are you tripping over your own feet?

How can shoes be part of your *identity*?

Notice, in the Foreward, my daughter mentioned my shoes. People are always watching.

Those archetypes in chapter four come out when I wear different shoes. Like my boots remind my warrior within me to "kick ass" and "I'm going to get through this." My pink pumps symbolize leaving my "pink print" or impression on the world. Because I give it so much meaning – I literally step into it. I own it.

When I surrendered my fear with losing my baggage, I stopped looking for what's missing and released my hold on the past. Instead, I reached out for my freedom in the promise of the future. I opened my heart to finding what truly matters— whether it's new experiences, deeper connections, or just the realization that I was more adaptable than I ever knew.

When I arrived at the airport, a regal and strong queen wearing my new shoes, the words, "We found your bag," greeted me at the ticket counter. "I'm going to be alright. I'm just moving forward," I affirmed to the ticket agent.

Now, with my two huge bags, twice the size of me, I headed home.

In Vegas, I saw my bags come around on the conveyer belt. Jet lagged, exhausted, and excited to see my kids, I was preparing to drag them off.

I looked up to see the man standing beside me smiling. Something about his eyes – I could tell he wasn't trying to pick me up. He said, "Would you like some help?" In his eyes, I immediately had the thought, "What a good man." ...And he was pretty hot.

That man... is now my husband.

We talked and laughed as he helped me lug this baggage outside. It turned out we lived less than two miles away from each other and had many of the same friends. Every time we tried to get together, we were both out of town. We laughed about living out of suitcases.

That day at the airport, I remember thinking after he left, "If I move to Encinitas, I might not get a chance to really know this guy." I lost my first and last month's deposit. I did what I had to do to stay in Las Vegas and I made it happen. I owned my worth. I wasn't thinking about all in my life that didn't work before. Instead of counting all the money I had lost in the past, I decided to earn more money now for the future.

Again, I surrendered. Was I scared? I was scared shitless. I felt alone. I just knew that we were going to be okay.

Even though there was a lot we didn't have. I had nothing financially at the time. Literally. I had three kids in private school $6000 a month. Car payment $750 a month. $3200 a month rent. New driver $225 a month insurance. No child support. I was freaking scared.

I didn't have my sparkle cowboy boots yet. I had ostrich boots that this man and his wife had given me. They cost $700 when he told me to go buy them as a thank you – I don't even remember what it was for. They were and are my reminder that people do care.

What do your shoes mean to you?

I often look to that time and wonder... did I have to let go and step into my queen shoes in order to be ready to meet Z that day in baggage claim?

These are absolutely ridiculous miracles of existence. They are precious rewards and the deepest *truths* of life. But you have to be *awake* to see the miracles.

Do you ride past the scenic views with your sights only on each next destination? Are you even looking out the window to appreciate what you've accomplished at all? Do you know where you're at on the map?

Creating a *Badass and Beautiful* life is all for nothing if you can't remember to enjoy and *deeply, and genuinely appreciate*, your present moment. Jump off the train and go see a stop—hang on for the ride! Embrace it all! Don't make space for more stuff, make space for more life. Look around at all you already have in your life and intentionally take your steps forward. *What are you most grateful for?*

Taking the time to be grateful is so important. Look around and really notice the gifts you already have—your body, the gift of vision and the ability to see a full spectrum of colors. The gift of touch. What does it feel like to receive another person's hand? The sweetness of a kiss? The warmth of a cozy bed? The scent of jasmine on the air? The sound of your child's laughter down the hall? The colorful sight of sunrise and sunset? The sensation of water on your skin?

Leading health experts have proven that regular gratitude has a direct impact on the feeling of life fulfillment and joy. Studies also show that your health will improve once you begin to take note of what is outside the windows of that train.

Sadly, so many people are sleepwalking, robotically moving from cube to cube—car, to office, to home, to bed and back again. There is a lot of work and no play or celebration.

For me, the fastest way to tap back into the genius (and magic) of life is to go into the wild. Nature reminds us of the intangible. When she reveals her endless bounties and awe-inspiring creations, she reminds us once again how to speak the language of mysteries.

I've learned so much from this wonderful woman who has come into my life. She has helped me to learn more deeply about why getting out into nature is so important. What I can predict from my time with Dr. Tamberly Conway is that our organic life will continue to mirror that of the macrocosm of Earth. Dr. Tamberly, is someone who understands this on a very deep level. She developed Forest Therapy programs for the US Forest Service, designed to reconnect people with nature at a deeper level of remembering; while also educating about the emotional, mental and physical benefits of nature. She champions the relationship of nature to human health and wellbeing. When the program funding was exhausted, she left the civil service and went into private practice with the tagline, "Get your nature dose on y'all." This Fall, Dr. Tamberly will be filming a documentary in South Korea to begin to tell the story of her "big idea," Nurturing Nature Lifelong Senior Communities. Her outcome is to provide support for elders, their loved ones, and caregivers; where care will be created around studies integrating intentional daily connection with nature that have proven to reduce cognition issues and other areas of decline related to aging.

When Dr. Tamberly first left the Forest Service, I know she had a start-stop process of deciphering where to invest her time, knowledge and resources for effecting the most positive change. I watched as she went through the process of discovery. She has been constantly questioning and re-inventing her approach until, finally, she realized the greatest need she could fulfill would be to increase the quality of life for elders in the US and beyond.

No matter how hard I might try, there is no way for me to predict exactly what my future holds, much less yours – but I do know from my observations of nature that there are cycles, seasons and patterns you can anticipate in life. Natural boundaries from which we can draw inspiration.

On this planet, we have seasons of the year. This metaphor can be applied to stages of life. Our relationships with others, even within the cycle of a business and sections of cities, and whole regimes go through seasons of re-birth all the way to death and back again.

My daughter was working on her senior essay after a friend of ours passed. In the essay she recounted the beauty in death. As a senior in high school, Asher is in the death of a season within her own life. She notes that death is often feared or avoided. A final and tragic ending, but after losing our dear friend over the summer, her perspective has begun to shift.

At the funeral, she witnessed the grace of someone embracing the remembrance of life lived perfectly imperfect with acceptance, not fear. Reflecting on the cycles of life and death more deeply, she observed beauty in the way everything, even life itself, ends. She realized that death is a natural part of the journey. A passage that makes life's moments all the more precious. With a calm understanding, she appreciated how fleeting time could be. The beauty of death, she learned, wasn't in the loss itself, but in the way it taught her to truly live, appreciate the gifts, and respect the souls who have passed before us.

Whatever season you're in right now, the path back to *Staying True* can be as easy as simply losing your baggage (death) and finding the right shoes (rebirth). Is there a part of this paradoxical badass and beautiful life you not yet embraced or released? Why?

A dear friend of mine of 30-plus years, the former Robbins Research Creative Vice-President, Pam Hendrickson, is known for saying, "The reward for a job well-done is more work." (It was actually her

Grandmother's quote—which adds even more validity as it has survived the ages).

Like I said earlier, this is *not* just another "shelf"-help program designed to keep you in an unrelenting holding pattern with the only hope for escape to attend a program.

Although there are benefits to courses and events (and I offer more than a few options if you're interested). That's not my *ultimate* mission with this book. I want to teach you to fish. I want you to step into *your* power, *for real*.

This takes discipline and application, which looks different, depending on where you're at in your lifecycle.

For me, when I am alive—dancing and flowing with life—I light up every archetype inside simultaneously. I am a beautiful hot mess of goddesses inside, alive, and ready to glide through life.

My Athena gets up on her horse, triumphant and firm. I might struggle to get my feet up in the stirrups, my hair might be a crazy mess, but I throw on my armor, pull up my tall boots, jump on the horse and go! Wild hair, don't care. My Hestia heart is in full gratitude, savoring every moment with my family and tribe. Coming home with the dust of my Athena ride still in my hair, I put on a flowy dress of Aphrodite, light some candles and dance in the dark. My friends know her, her process may not make any sense to anyone else, but it doesn't matter because I understand her perfectly. She makes up new moves and each of her bright colors is on full display.

This wild hot mess means I'm *alive*.

What does it mean to you, to be alive? For me, I find this place when I'm in tune with how special all the little things are—food on my table, safety in my home, the ability to love and be loved. I feel deep gratitude for it all. That recognition lights me up from the inside out so brightly that everything shines.

What about you? Who are you when you are most *alive*?

Every sad love song reminds us, we don't know what we have until it's gone. In the day-to-day of living, we miss all the miracles right under our nose. The one major pitfall that blinds us the "not-enough-ness" game. Swimming in a constant feeling of lack. We constantly fear we are not "enough," and in order to know we are truly

loved completely, we think we need to be more...
and more... and more. But I know from reading
countless surveys and speaking around the world
that people are tired of comparing themselves to
where they think they *should* be by now.

This is my take on that rabbit hole—the world will
keep asking more from you until you feel like a
worn-out rag. It's not enough to be a mom and to
have a successful career. It's not enough to show
up and just be a good human. My advice is to step
back and redefine the game so that the goals
you're striving for are on your *own* terms (boundaries). Remove any paraments that set you up to
feel like you are letting others down.

I call this being "happily discontent." This concept
creates space to grow, but simultaneously allows
me happiness in the *process*. I balance that sense
of striving and growing with overflowing gratitude and giving.

In this way, there is no longer lack. "Happily
Discontent" honors the paradox of being present
(and fully enjoying). My biggest drive to expand
my reach, impact and bottom line is to be well-
equipped to help other people and animals when
it matters most.

What about you? What is driving *you* for more?

This is a good place to go back to your compass. Pause, find your way and ask yourself some truth-setting, boundary building questions. Go outside and look around—find something miraculous within a single blade of grass, a child's smile, or a bird on a branch.

That same miracle is you, and now that you have this *truth* within you, you can't unknow it. Truth doesn't waiver or suffer from self-doubt because deep down, you *know* how unstoppable you are.

Whatever it is – know there is a purpose.

There is a purpose for every person you meet. Some are there to test you, some will use you, some will teach you, and some will bring out the best in you.

Beyond my larger events, what really makes my heart sing is deep relationships. Ones made within the intimate retreats for my special TLC Mastermind groups—36 women who are committed to helping each other succeed. This week was such a beautiful week. We were celebrating one day—the next day praying for healing for somebody's husband. We were cheering people on as they took the stage and encouraging others as they healed from surgery. We are living life in full techno-color together. It is scary, but exciting.

At one of my recent retreats, we invited an amazing mother and daughter team Rima Thundercloud and Phaedra Mog—to join us.

They have and shared their beautiful lineage with us, as well as the ability to help others find their truth, to hear their own voice of intuition and inner wisdom. Their process resonates with me as both authentic and sacred.

In Sedona during a ritual, Rima Thundercloud gifted me with a hand-made drum. She explained that she had made this drum several months earlier, not knowing who the owner was, but after meeting me, she determined that she'd, in fact, made it for me—but we still had to test it make sure she was right.

She proceeded to put tobacco on top of the drum and then softly began to beat it. With each beat, the tobacco moved into a perfect line, moving toward me. She told me that the energy would only move toward me if there was space for it, if my truth was real (and not from ego). This is what defined the drum as meant for me.

I was so honored to receive this gift and now keep it an arm's length away, in my office. To me it's a symbol of the work I've done to *Stay True* (again and again).

Deep down somewhere, you *know* that you were designed to shine, you *know* that you are here on this planet for more than a mundane existence, and you *know* that by simply being alive, you are living a miraculous existence.

No more sleeping beauty.

The world needs us to wake up, step into our power and *stay awake*. It needs us to offer up the truth of our voice and our wisdom. The Badass and Beautiful Woman belongs to us all, and with all of the unrest and uncertainty in the world, we need her (your) intuition, your sense of justice and integrity, your medicine in the form of song and poetry, your healing dignity and sage wisdom.

People speak of "the divine feminine spirit" (another way to explain your Queen, she's waiting) I asked Phaedra Mog to help me explain it. The feminine is nurturing to all; the feminine is inclusive; the feminine feeds and fortifies soul, body, and mind; the feminine is resilience; the feminine is courage; the feminine is fierce to be effective in the moment, but not rigid, it flows on to overcome obstacles; the feminine is connected to spirit; the feminine forgives; the feminine heals; the feminine listens empathically to understand; the feminine is a vessel for light and energy, a portal for life—not only in childbirth, but in communities, companies, and families. Women conduct what is needed to make life happen. From all of this, there is a strength greater than any force that burns from the inside. Our greatest power is in giving from within with a steady and constant burn like a fire against Winter's cold.

Please don't hold back.

Who represents the badass and beautiful women of today for you? Who is this in your life? Maybe you are sparked alive by the light in a picture of you at 5-years-old or by Iris, that 102-year-old designer I mentioned, the one who lived-out-loud by wearing chunky bracelets, bright patterns, and big glasses. It's never too early nor too late to awaken *your* wild badass and beautiful woman.

Free your inner goddesses, all of them. And keep singing *your* chord, that unique song only you can sing, as loudly, clearly and cleanly as you possibly can. As I said in an earlier chapter, Wayne Dyer says, "Don't let the music die within you."

What shoes do you need to slip on to wake her? Give yourself permission to *trust* the voice inside yourself. What music, art, people, nature is needed to help her wake up and enjoy this train ride of life? The discovery and re-discovery to find your color-outside-the-lines unique purpose and badass and beautiful woman voice is part of the beautiful wild ride itself.

In the space below and before moving forward, create a symbol (like my shoes are for me) or drawing—some sort of visual representation of your badass and beautiful woman self. It doesn't have to be pretty, and don't be afraid to color outside the lines. Whatever you create doesn't even have to make "sense." Challenge yourself to get out of your own way to simply let it flow.

8

ORDER IT UP: YOU ARE A MAGNET

Once upon a time a sadly neglected woman dies and goes to heaven. She is promptly met at the pearly gates by the ethereal aura of St. Peter, who says, "Welcome and enjoy! You can do absolutely whatever you'd like."

After walking around and exploring heaven for a few days, she finds a large and mysterious closed door. Curious, she opens it up and goes inside. There she finds a big room with giant boxes beautifully wrapped and sealed with magically woven gold ribbon. As she gets closer, she notices that every box has a name on it. Intrigued she begins looking to see for a box that might be hers. Eventually she finds one with her name neatly typed on top.

Just as she is about to tear open the box, St. Peter finds her here. "What are doing?" he asks.

"I found this magical box with my name on it, and I was just about to open it. Presents here in heaven must contain incredible gifts. I can't wait to see what's inside."

"Ah," said St. Peter with a glimmer in his eye.

"What you find in that box won't mean much to you here. That box contains everything you *could* have had on Earth if you would have just asked for it."

With an astonished stare, she puts the box aside and decides not to open it after all.

This wild beautiful world, arm in arm, with its wild beautiful ride is full of abundance. There is opportunity *everywhere*, and scarcity stems only from blocks and barricades of our own making.

In Quantum Physics and Religion, the theory is that we are all one. The energy we all source from is one light. If you watch a sunbeam fall through the window, it is impossible to separate each particle with our eye. If you take a glass and fill it water from the ocean, that water is still a part of the ocean. Similarly, if you take a piece of rock from a mountain, it is still the mountain.

Imagine a boulder falling away from a mountain. Once the boulder lands and breaks away, we can clearly see that it still "mountain," even though it begins to call itself "boulder" as it falls to the ground. Yet all of its contents and at the core of its DNA, the boulder is 100 percent still mountain.

It only begins to differ from its source when it forgets where it came from. That's where who you choose for your tribe matters. There are studies that prove our DNA actually mimics that of its surroundings.

In this way, we are still as divine as the Source we stem from—whatever you consider that to be. We're only separate from that Source because we forget we are made of the same ingredients and that our DNA contains this ultimate truth.

Furthermore, the magnitude and infinite power of the universe, in whatever words you use to label this energy, is *on your side*. In the words of

The Talmud, "Every blade of grass has its Angel that bends over it and whispers, 'Grow, grow.'"

Just as the boulder hears the call of the mountain and a drop of water hears the song of the ocean, if you slow down enough to listen, you can hear the light of your connected soul. The genius of living your *Badass and Beautiful* life opens up a thread-line with your highest self, which magnetizes you toward your "true" course, or purpose. As I explained at the very start of this book—the Earth is a gigantic magnet, and so are *you*.

In ancient stories the spirit of the Wild Woman can be compared to that of a wolf—it is revered with great power. Why? Because the wolf represents a spirit who will not be caged. It is the archetype of her own spirit.

When united with *your divine truth*, you too, are like a wolf. You just need apply that wild wisdom (your own remembering) to your own soul. Listen closely to find your rhythm. *No one* can turn it off—unless you stifle your own soul.

To that end, this chapter is called "Order It Up" because I believe that once you tap into your truth, you tap into your highest self and you reconnect to Source. From here, you just need to ask for what you want in life.

It doesn't have to be profound. It goes like this – what you want more of in your life you will attract. At my events I often tell this story about how I told my husband how much I love flowers and asked him to send them to me. His response—sending me flowers *every single Friday*.

When I was married to my kids' father, I wanted so much to be loved by a really nice guy. This is where archetypes come in. In my world, the archetype of a "nice guy" needed to be married to a "low maintenance woman." Flowers were "extra."

At one time, I actually told him, "I don't need flowers." Which to him meant, I didn't want them at all. So, in all the years we were married, he honored the archetype that I had told him he was married to.

In the end, I never had flowers bought for me because I was showing up as a person who didn't want flowers. In short, I didn't ask for them. The reason I didn't ask for them was because I was playing small and not owning my truth.

In reality, I really want flowers. Is it the flowers I want? No, in truth—it's the old-fashioned, "thought that counts" adage.

For 13 years, I've received flowers on Friday from Z. Remember, I told him, "I'm the catch of the century." The "catch of the century" must be treasured in a different way than someone who has the "low maintenance" archetype.

In my heart, I value most is that every Friday he remembers me. He makes it a priority to make sure a flower is received before sunset. Sometimes it might be a flower drawn in the sand or a picture of a flower in our yard, but there is a flower on Friday without fail. Before any flowers could happen, I had to show up as my true self and ask for what I *really* want in life and my relationship.

Let me tell you, it lights me up, *every time*.

It really is that simple. Use your voice and ask for what you want and truthfully OWN YOUR WORTH. Show up as your whole self aways. Like Asher said in the foreward, "remain authentic to yourself even when others would want you to hide."

Since I've been sharing this story at my events, many other women told me that they've started asking for flowers too… and they've been receiving them too.

I like to visualize Fridays now as a massive, colorful, beautiful shared bouquet. A collective gift of flowers is beautiful to imagine. The energy and aliveness must make the heavens, shine brighter every Friday, lit up by so many women in my circle.

What about you—what do you *really* want? To order it up, like writing a list for Santa, you need to get clear about what to ask for.

In the labyrinth of life, many of us wander around without truly asking for what we want. But what if I told you that the keys to your wildest dreams are in your hands? It's all about getting the clarity and the courage to ask.

A decade ago, my friend joined a mastermind group called "Ladies Who Launch," a dynamic incubator for women striving to turn their visions into reality. For six weeks, they met, strategized, and supported each other as they worked to bring their ideas to life. By the final meeting, she felt confident and prepared to embark on her new business venture. Each member was asked to write out and read a vision for their future. My friend's vision was practical and detailed, laying out the steps she needed to take. But there was one line, almost an afterthought, that caught the group's attention: "...and someone to share all of this with."

After she finished reading, the leader honed in on that last part. "Let's talk about that," she said. My friend blushed, wishing she had kept that thought to herself, but the group encouraged her to explore it further.

One of the women, an interior designer with a deep understanding of Feng Shui, offered a suggestion: "Write down the specific qualities you want in a partner, find a photo that represents that, and place it behind a piece of art you look at regularly." It was an unusual request, but with nothing to lose, my friend decided to give it a try. She made the list, then leafed through a stack of "Outside" magazines, finding a photo that felt right—a man who embodied the traits she desired. She tucked it behind a painting in her living room and let it go, trusting the process.

Two weeks later, a friend invited her on a last-minute ski trip. Despite the late season and the so-so snow conditions, she decided to go. There was only one other person on the trip—a man who looked eerily like the image she had placed behind her painting. At first, she chalked it up to coincidence, but as the trip unfolded, she realized he possessed every quality she had written down. On the last day of the trip, he turned to her and said, "I made a list of all the qualities I'm looking for in a partner, and you're everything on my list."

They've been together for 15 years now, living in the Rocky Mountains, married for over a decade, and still sharing adventures as best friends. What if it really is this simple? What if clarity and asking are the keys to manifesting the life you truly want?

Consider the story of Lauren Finkelstein, the founder of SaveOnePerson.org, a nonprofit that helps connect people in need of kidney donors. When Lauren attended one of my Manifest Magnificent courses, she was navigating deep emotional challenges. She had lost her father in 1998, survived a suicide bomber, and felt a burning desire to use her television production skills to help others.

Lauren was clear on her mission, but she needed guidance on how to bring it to life. Together, we worked on answering two crucial questions: 1) Who are you, really? and 2) Where are you going? Through the process of creating a Manifestation

Board, she honed in on her vision with laser-like precision. She asked herself, "What would a queen do?" and then acted accordingly, stepping into her power with confidence and clarity.

That clarity allowed Lauren to manifest incredible outcomes: she developed an app, authored a book, and recently saw a significant increase in donations for SaveOnePerson.org, all while navigating personal challenges related to addiction and divorce. This year, for the first time, her donations began to rise steadily—first $1, then $25, $50, $100. And just this week, she woke up to a $1,000 donation. Lauren Finkelstein saves lives because she dared to ask and remained committed to her vision.

When you're clear about where you're going, your mind becomes a powerful magnet, attracting the people, opportunities, and resources you need to achieve your dreams. It's as if the universe conspires in your favor, delivering exactly what you need when you need it most. Sometimes, it comes effortlessly, like a flowers on Fridays. Other times, it requires persistent effort, but the results are worth it.

The message here is simple: Get clear on what you want, then ask for it with unwavering belief.

The universe is abundant and generous, but it responds to clarity and action. So, what do you want? Write it down. Speak it out loud. Visualize it every day. And then, order it up.

Your life is a masterpiece in the making, and you are the artist. Every stroke, every choice, every ask shapes your reality. So, step into your power, embrace your worth, and create a life that not only fulfills you but also inspires others to do the same. Remember, you are unstoppable when you align your vision with your actions. The world is waiting for your brilliance—now go out there and shine. What will you order up?

STEP 3: TRUE VOICE

9

OCEAN OF EMOTION

History has shown us that one badass and beautiful woman, a steadfast, unrelenting soul with her eyes set on an uncompromising vision, can shift the world. She does so by standing up for justice and love, with an unreasonable dose of wild passion. Now, if one woman can hold the light as a teacher, healer, artist, and warrior for good in the world, imagine what a "ride or die" crew of such women could spark. Although we thrive as individuals, a tribe of aligned women focused on lifting each other up is the heart of the entire planet—maybe even the universe. A group of women living their truth at their highest potential is one of nature's most sacred gifts.

A tribe is there for you when you cannot go further. When you need to rest, to pause, to be encouraged and uplifted, a true friend is there to hold your weight. You can pass them your baton to carry on when you can't. These are the people who have your back and bring you back to your true *identity*. A true tribe leads you back to yourself. As we discussed earlier, science and spirituality agree, "You become your environment."

This chapter brings us full circle. No matter where you end up or how far apart you are, a true tribe can reawaken your heart and bring you back home to your truth. A true friend can sing the song of your soul back to you when you've forgotten the words.

Even if you don't have this sort of friend in your circle right now, I guarantee that if you are fully staying true to yourself, that friend will find you—just like a magnet. And if you don't believe me, consider this an open invitation to join my tribe. I'm serious. Go to lorenlahav.com or find my Facebook group and jump in. We've got your back.

I've been fortunate enough to build several strong tribes over the years. Even so, there are certain people who stand out above and beyond. There are those who "sing your song back to you," and then there are those who lift you up even beyond themselves to shine.

Have you ever had that sort of friend? One who saw more potential in you than you saw in yourself? The friend who has done this for me, over and over again, through each decade of my life—20s, 30s, 40s, 50s, and now 60s—is an amazing soul and beautiful badass named Mary Glorfield.

Not everyone gets me. I'm known as a whirlwind of energy, a hurricane, or the part of river rapids that might throw you out of the boat. But my friends, the ones who really understand me, call me the Ocean of Emotion. I feel everything—deeply. I don't care if the way I live looks chaotic or messy to the outside observer. To me, it just means I'm living fully. It means that I'm alive. And if I'm being honest, I see those people on the outside—observing, judging, and not understanding me—as emotionally constipated life dabblers.

Mary somehow always understood me, even when others in our shared workspace didn't. She's the one who advocated and pushed for me to be the facilitator to launch the program for Tony Robbins' Life Mastery event. She's the one who championed me to lead events for him all over the world. And since I've moved on and created my own events, she's continually connected me with resources and growth opportunities. Through all of the years (four decades of time), I actually feel like she wants my success even more than her own.

This is rare and extraordinary. It's giving just to give, without expectation of anything in return. It's looking for the best in someone and cheering for what you see endlessly. Has anyone ever done this for you? Who believes in you? Who are your cheerleaders? Who do you lean on when you're not strong?

A few years ago, someone came along giving me the opportunity to give back to someone in the same way Mary has mentored me all these years. Imagine a corporate events planner who had built a solid reputation for orchestrating large-scale events with precision and flair. When COVID hit, everything changed. This special tribe member of mine is Dancia. She was a new mom right when COVID kicked off.

She found herself adapting to the new realities of my world, helping me plan a virtual gathering, a

5-Day Challenge and then, as we started to "open up again," a Badass and Beautiful event.

Seeing me take risks with my own money as an entrepreneur is eye-opening for Danica. Despite the uncertainty, she and I have rocked Own Your Worth together.

She reminds me of who I was 20 years ago. She's not just a helper; she's a cornerstone, someone who you can always count on to get things done right. Whether it's organizing an event, managing schedules, or solving unexpected problems, she handles it all with a calm demeanor and a warm smile. Her customer service approach is extraordinary. Danica's presence is reassuring, her work ethic unmatched, and her attention to detail is exemplary.

Do you have a circle of peers, a mastermind, or a personal Board of Directors? Perhaps you have a loose circle of friends, but have you specifically asked them to be a part of your official support team?

It's rare to find someone who combines such competence with genuine kindness and a positive attitude as Veronica, my stylist. She travels with me to events. Not only makes the time away from my family easier, but also brighter. Having her around feels like having a secret weapon—a blend of wisdom, skill, and heart that makes everything run smoothly. She truly is the person everyone wishes they had by their side. Some people on my team call her my Fairy Godmother.

She is complimented by Juliana, my photographer. This momma bear embodies the essence of a faithful sidekick—reliable, versatile, and endlessly resourceful. She's the kind of person who always knows what needs to be done, often before anyone else does. Her ability to capture people's essence and brand with grace is nothing short of impressive.

My photographer and stylist are not just the people who make me look good—we love supporting one another. A friend of mine the other day just said, "You are right Loren! Why not take my bestie who does hair and makeup with me to my event?! She will make sure I look good and we will have as much fun as you do with Veronica doing Facebook LIVES after 17-hour days eating at late-night diners!"

Everyone is different, and we find and create our tribes in different ways. It would be nice if we had a "Tinder Tribe" app to do it for us. (Royalties, please, if you run with this idea!)

With this year building my companies especially—I've been grateful for people who have come into my life. Vanessa, is a member of my TLC membership. She thought she was joining a "club" to be a part of during her retirement and she ended up running my company as the CEO and starting a wellness spa franchise, Stay True Wellness Spa, with me and another partner and TLC sister, Stephanie Karlstad.

Be careful if you come to Las Vegas, Marissa is the Chief Operating Officer of STCP, thanks to a lunch "catch up." One day she called to let me know she and moved to town and the next thing you know; she is making business cards and planning Scopes of Work for the agency.

And you would agree if you met her! Imagine, someone who has spent years behind the scenes crafting award-winning shows with an impeccable eye for detail. Her career has been marked by a relentless pursuit of excellence, where every frame, every line of dialogue, and every nuance of production is scrutinized until it's perfect. Her dedication to her craft has earned her a reputation as a consummate professional, someone whose work consistently garners critical acclaim and industry accolades.

As you build your tribe or acknowledge who's already there, perhaps it's even more interesting to point the mirror at ourselves: Who do you support? Who do you look out for? Who do you lift up and promote? And how do you go about doing so?

I have something I call my "Nifty Fifty." (It's actually grown to "Nifty 500" and now "Nifty 5000.") It's the 50+ people who I look out for—the ones I'm committed to supporting and championing. There are many ways we can help each other; most of them are pretty simple—a shout-out on social media, purchasing the products and services our friends offer, and providing referrals are all solid ways to express professional support. You can also take the time to really listen and be a big ear, offer up your favorite resources and advice. Often, the best gift we can offer our tribe is to simply reach out with a hug or smile.

You see, this ocean of emotion isn't just about feeling deeply. It's about connecting deeply, living deeply, and ultimately loving deeply. When you find your tribe and embrace the power of connection, you're not just lifting yourself up—you're lifting the world. So, go out there, find your tribe, and let's make some waves together.

Let me tell you something profound yet simple: The people in your life are like the roots of trees in a forest—connected, interdependent, and essential for your growth. We might stand tall as individuals, but beneath the surface, our roots intertwine with those of our tribe, creating a network of support and strength.

Wayne Dyer once said, "Change the way you look at things, and the things you look at change." Now, imagine if you changed the way you look at your tribe. Not just as a collection of friends, but as your personal ecosystem, each member contributing to your life in ways you might not always see. You see, just as trees in a forest share nutrient through their roots, so too do we share our energy, wisdom, and love with those closest to us.

But here's the thing: just as some roots grow stronger, some wither away—that's okay. People come into your life for a reason, a season, or a lifetime. What matters is recognizing who your true tribe is—those who are there for you, who support you without expecting anything in return, and who lift you higher even when you feel like you can't go on.

Take my "Nifty 50," for instance. It's a group that started small and has now grown to include hundreds, even thousands, of people. But it's not just about the numbers; it's about the energy. Some people have been in my life for decades, like Mary, who has always seen the potential in me, even when I didn't see it myself. Others come and go, and that's okay too. Tribes are fluid, just like life.

But here's the real magic: as you grow, so does your tribe. You attract people who resonate with the energy you put out into the world. So, take a moment today to reflect on who's in your tribe. Then, take a moment to ensure that you are showing up as the person you want to be. Now notice, who are the people that make you feel alive, that challenge you, that help you become the best version of yourself? And equally important, who are the people that drain you, that make you feel small or insignificant?

As my daughter Asher so wisely pointed out, you don't have to tolerate people who make you feel like crap. Life's too short for that. Surround yourself with those who bring out the best in you, and who you can support in return. This is your tribe, your forest of strength.

Now, let's get practical. Do the people in your life know how much you appreciate them? When was the last time you told them? Don't wait for a eulogy to share the remarkable things you see in those you love. Tell them now. Lift them up with your words and your actions.

And if you're feeling alone, know this: the right people will find you. But you've got to be true to yourself first. Show up as the best version of you, and your tribe will naturally form around that energy. And if you need a place to start, join us. I've got a group of like-minded, professional, con-tribution-focused, heart-centered souls out there owning their truth and making it happen in the world who are ready to welcome you with open arms.

Remember, just like the trees, we are stronger together. Let's nurture those roots, celebrate our connections, and grow into the incredible, inter-twined forest that we are meant to be.

You are a unique facet of the universal diamond, each of us multi-faceted in our own space, dis-tinctly reflecting the brilliance of life. When we fail to show up as our best selves, we dim the light of the entire community, disrupting the harmony we are meant to create together. Imagine if a single cell in your body didn't fulfill its purpose—the entire organism could falter. That's how critical your role is. You are a vital note in the symphony of the universe, essential on your own—yet intricately woven into the greater harmony.

As I always say, "There will never be a perfect moment—stop waiting and start doing." The world needs more of you, more of your truth. And as you embrace this, your tribe will resonate with you, amplifying your song as you amplify theirs. Together, you'll create a powerful chorus of truth and purpose.

Take a moment to reflect:

In your community, who do you believe in?

Who inspires you, and why?

What gifts do you see in them?

How do you share your gifts with the world?

What groups or activities in your community resonate with your passions?

Where can you find like-minded individuals, online or in person?

Is there a group or organization you've been meaning to reconnect with?

The voices you uplift and the communities you engage with can transform not only your life but the lives of those around you. Consider:

How can you elevate the voices that inspire you?

What strengths do you want to develop within yourself, and where can you do that locally?

How can you show up for those who need it?

Who is your tribe of five—the "board of directors" you can turn to, no matter what? Reach out to them and let them know their value. If you don't have a tribe, now is the time to manifest one.

Ask yourself:

What traits do you need in a friend? (Good listener, funny, shares stories, spiritual, grounded, healer, nurturer, etc.)

What archetypes would your friends embody, and how would they interact with yours?

What kind of work would your friends do, and where could you meet them?

Remember, your community is a reflection of you. When you show up as your highest self, you give others permission to do the same. Let's create the tribe that will sing your song and uplift the world.

10

TRIBE:
THE GOLDEN THREAD

Have you ever heard of a totem pole? They are from all over the world. In the US, the Pacific North-West Native Americans use totems to represent families. They are logs carved with birds and animals that symbolize the different family members.

Just like these relics, we metaphorically stand on the shoulders of the remarkable women who came before us. Something to never be forgotten.

Who is someone from the past that has made a difference in who you are?

In some cultures, a totem could be one sculpture that is thought of as family's guardian, also symbolic reminder of a member of the family tree who has passed on.

What animal represents where you are going to be? A phoenix, eagle, dog more playful.

Let's cut through the noise right now. You are either reading for inspiration on the fence – wondering what your next move is going to be.

Joan of Arc, born to a peasant family, became the savior of the French by helping King Charles save France from British rule by riding out straight into the battlefield with her banner trailing behind her—at age 17.

Messy-haired and wild-hearted, Amelia Earhart, is known as the first woman to fly solo across the Atlantic, regularly broke the "rules" on what women were expected to be and do. She was too busy building rollercoaster-like ramps off her family's roof to "act like lady." After serving as a nurse during World War I, she paid for flying lessons by working for a telephone company and driving trucks. Why? She knew that action speaks louder than any expectation that society could place on her.

Another power house: Mother Teresa. She redefined service, "None of us can do great things, but we can do small things with great love." It is not about grand gestures – it is about taking the first step with conviction.

Here's the truth – it only takes 25 percent of a population to reshape a society and reach the tipping point. That's all it takes for a minority to shift behavior for the majority.

Your actions, yes YOU can be the very one that tips the scales.

You think the ancient women didn't know this? They did. When throughout history have recognized that when united, power is amplified to change the world.

Small things done with true passion create a fork in the great river of life.

Why are you not doing the same?

In the world where the divine feminine has been repressed. I have created this space for the last 25-years. To not just talk – but to ask. Not to survive – but to thrive. To honor each other. To blaze a trail that others can follow.

You have two choices right now. You can stay in your comfort zone waiting for the perfect moment and the perfect circumstances or the perfect you to arrive. Or you can decide right now in this moment – imperfections and all to take action and make the difference that you know you are here to make.

You have a golden thread that has connected you to every woman who has come before you. A legacy of strength, resilience, and wisdom. It is time to grab that thread and pull yourself into the light.

Don't just read about the women who change the world, be one.

This is our legacy. As women, this is our *collective truth*. The Celts have a symbol for the maiden, the mother, and the crone. Great-grandmothers, grandmothers, mothers and daughters together—linking the wonders and innocence of youth to the wisdom of the elders. Biologically, when you think about it – it all makes sense. We once were held by the womb of another within the womb of the first. Grandmother held mother, held grand-daughter.

With what we know about morphic resonance, if accessed, this combined strength can circulate through the heart of every woman—empowering the Wild Woman in us all.

I call this inherent potential our Golden Thread. This thread that connects each of us to the next throughout history.

In both legend and recorded time, women have been coming together to support and amplify each other. In ancient Greece, there were the Oracles. The *curanderos* of Peru were medicine women who would meet to share tinctures, recipes and trades.

In modern days, we have lost touch with this valued tradition. Yet, I've noticed in these last two years, a call has begun to sound, drawing us back together in some ways—women's circles are on the rise. The sacred tribe of sisterhood is experiencing a Spring.

Even when we gather, do we recognize our own power?

Through my events and Mastermind Circles, I've been making a point to nurture this legacy. In doing so, it gives us insight to many other useful truths. Our bodies are connected to Earth's shifting tides and seasons. We literally, move and flow with her. Therefore, as living example of both art and science intertwined, the mysteries of nature make sense somewhere inside us—if we listen.

There are common themes. As the maiden, we embody Spring. Here we celebrate the blessing of new life. The gift is not just in newness, it is in perspective—one that stems from the DNA of the past. We also compare ourselves to others, balancing expectations, and work-life boundaries test our *truth*.

Too often, we dismiss the thoughts and questions of the young, labeling them as immature or inexperienced. As youth ourselves, we may even undervalue our own voices. But truly listening to children, teenagers, and young adults is essential. The gift of youth lies in its vibrant connection to the divine, offering fresh perspectives unclouded by the complexities of adulthood. If we hold space to really hear them, we open ourselves to insights that can illuminate the blind spots holding us back. The phrase "from the mouths of babes" reminds us that sometimes the simplest, most profound truths come from the youngest among us, offering the shifts in perspective needed to break through our human barriers.

As the mother, we shine and *give endlessly* like Summer's sun. This selfless season is how we pass on the intangible wisdom of limitless love. This is something that women uniquely offer up. It is as if in giving birth (be it to an idea, company, or a human), we not only create something physical, but we also create (and recreate) a shield of love.

In many ancient texts and practices, love is the center of our existence. In fact, love, may very well be the glue that holds the entire universe together. The mother holds the depth of love's power. In listening to, or more-so, holding space, to receive the emotions and feelings of mothers as they sit in circle with us, we have access to their "love glue." Like an energetic salve that serves as both a shield and an antibody to heal the wounds around us, we can then put it to work in the world.

As the mentor, we become masters of efficiency—focusing on the vital necessities of life. If you cut out all the bullsh#$ what is left? Just as Fall sheds her leaves and goes dormant, at the mentor season of life, we shed the things and people that don't serve us. We gain power in unlearning the dogmas and societal expectations that are no longer necessary. Within the circle, these women remind us not to take ourselves (or anyone else) too seriously. They see clearly where we are wasting time, or effort, or heart. With their candid, direct advice, they help us laugh, mostly at ourselves. *Staying True* to purpose, health, self-advocacy and voice. Our *truth* takes the shape of shared wisdom, coaching and mentorship.

As the elder, we can share how to survive any of Winter's harshest blows—with grace. The elder has seen it all, lived through it all, and made peace with it all. She understands that life moves through its seasons consistently and that in doing so, there is a balance to it all. She has witnessed the bliss of a rise and the pity of a fall, many times over, in both herself and those around her. She understands the paradox of both joy and sorrow. She sees that, in fact, an understanding of true joy would not even be possible without the contrast of sorrow.

In this way, she understands that life's wild ride speaks in riddles. And that the meaning of it all is never as complicated as we think. When we invite her to sit with us in circle, she tells us these things, without necessarily saying so, by flashing a gleam through her ever-sparkling eyes. *Staying True* shows up with confidence in freedom; it resounds in the legacy she wishes to leave for others.

Here's the thing, at every stage in life we face unique challenges that test our *truth*. Whether you are a teen navigating *identity*, a mother embracing chaos of love, or an elder sharing the wisdom of a lifetime – *Staying true* isn't a solo journey, it is a collective one. Our golden thread connects us all. Linking our individual stories into a tapestry of purpose and strength. When we listen to each other and support each other we thrive.

I received this message at 1:21 in the morning as we are making the final edits to this book from Dena, one of my TLC ladies, "Loren I love how much you give and pour into others always without bias – even though you have your own political opinions you *stay true* to yourself with an open heart and respect for everyone. You manage to remain neutral, focusing on being authentic without belittling others. You listen for crucial issues, channeling them into something positive. You live in a way that is all about value, so that we can also all positively affect the world. Focusing our energy on unity, peace, and love we are able to see how much we have in common and it makes all the difference in the relationships of our collective. Thank you."

That is quite possibly one of the best compliments I've ever received.

Everything I do is the result of my truth manifested with the help of my tribe. People come and go. Over the years it has been all about a force of good. Those good ripples beyond around the globe. As this movement grows, forces combine and that is why the impact is growing.

This is an invitation. Come dance around our bonfire with us. Let's gather under the stars. Let's be badass and beautiful – lifting each other up and howling at the moon. Whether you join ours' or create your own – know this – if you *stay true*. You will find your tribe. It's a super power part of your DNA and that golden thread.

This book, my True Legacy Collective and my events are the result of my *truth* and the collaboration of my tribe to manifest its realization with me. I value the women in my tribe for reasons beyond words. The journey to where I am now in this very moment was in itself healing, cathartic, and only made possible because of the bond (golden thread of shared purpose) strung connecting each of us within our tribe.

A study from the University of Cambridge, calls this, "The Art of Living together." It shows that small communities thrive and have distinct impacts on the lives of those within them.

On your wild journey, I believe that the invitation, opportunity and desire to tap back into the power of our generations exists. We just need use it.

11

PASSING THE BADASS & BEAUTIFUL TORCH

Let's have a real talk about taking action. Not in two years or when you finally have time – but right now. Because if we are honest, time isn't waiting for anyone and neither should your dreams.

When I think about honoring the sacred feminine, my Mom is the first person who comes to mind. She is from a generation when all the fluff of life was strip away leaving nothing but pure, unfiltered wisdom. Her lessons are absolute gold.

I owe everything I am to my parents. Growing up my Mom and Dad taught me the values that shaped my life Resilience, perseverance, reciprocity, philanthropy, spirituality, and above all—gratitude.

My parents didn't talk the talk – they walked the walk. Those footsteps became the path I followed.

Her guiding principle? Unwavering commitment to her husband. Even now she describes Dad as, "A wonderful, wonderful, wonderful man. Very kind and intelligent—everybody loved him. He was so good."

My Mom's life is a Masterclass in "I'll try that." The pillars would be: Hard Work, Ingenuity, and Giving Grace and Gratitude to G-d.

She came from humble beginnings. She was born in California, and grew up in Las Vegas, Los Angeles, and Albuquerque. She worked in a record store and was as a result in the Hollywood "in crowd" while living in Beverly Hills and attending UCLA before she met my Dad. She follows this up with a disclaimer, "It was fun and I had some interesting relationships, but it was nothing special."

She shares she was always a dreamer. Which is a pillar lesson in itself, to "Dream." But, the difference that hits home for me is that her hopes and dreams were that my brother and I would fulfill our dreams. That we would live a happy, successful, and healthy life—that because we have fulfilled these dreams for ourselves, we have in-turn fulfilled her dreams.

"Hard Work and Diligence" are how she defines my brother and I as well as her parents. This value lead to owning an import company with her sister that took her all over Europe. She enjoyed the work she had in her retail/import business immensely; however, in the end, the time she had to spend away from home over-shadowed the joy of the endeavor (her first love being her family).

"Give Grace and Gratitude to God." My Mom came from humble beginnings. Her parents worked hard. When you ask her about her early life – she doesn't feel there is a lot to share; however, when you ask her about my brother and I she lights up, "I was blessed with my two wonderful children. They are 1-year and 2-days apart. I've always joked this is what "Unplanned parenthood" looks like."

"Give to those less fortunate." She shares that at one time she had 7-dogs. She jokes that she was a dog hoarder because stray dogs have a way of finding her. She follows this story with the memory that as a family we always did "charity work." I've mentioned giving back was a cardinal principle in our home.

Here's the thing—just as my mom did for me—you have the power to pay it forward. As parents this comes naturally. And yet, for all of us, the art of passing the torch (to anyone) is one of the most fulfilling principles of *being alive*. In fact, I believe we are wired to *share* deep within our cells.

I'd like to offer some full disclosure. I'd like to say I wrote this entire book all by myself, but I didn't. In fact, I leaned into two of the smartest brainy, creative, and downright brilliant women I've met. I might be super simple in my approach, but these two bring depth, insight, and a whole lot of genius to the table. Two close friends, (Catherine "Catie" Krueger Sullivan and Jill Marek) are my *Stay True* book team. Their energy and wisdom and badass and beautiful linage are woven into this book as well.

Watch how the thread unfolds. I interviewed both of them to understand the gifts passed on to them. Think of the generations of badass and beautiful women that lead to this page before you. Let's integrate what we've learned together. What Compass Rose did their mothers use on their journeys that ultimately helped shape these two women? What questions did they have to Inquire of themselves in order to stay the course of their True North? What Rituals did they have? What Boundaries did they keep? How did the importance of Tribe show up in their lives?

In the life of Pamela Hicks Krueger, the 13th female Naval Aviator and one of the first female commercial pilots in the US, we see the Compass Rose. The power of inquiry, the grounding in rituals, the setting of boundaries, and the importance of tribe.

It all began with a powerful question, posed by her mother Janet Brakel Hicks: "Pam, what would make your life fuller right now?" That inquiry lit a spark within Pam, who had given up on her dream of flying because the world told her "girls don't fly." Her mother's question gave her the courage to respond, "Mom, I want to fly." That simple, but profound answer changed the course of her life. Janet immediately enrolled Pam in aviation school, setting her on a trailblazing path.

Pam's Ritual was simple but unwavering: "Just keep flying." She earned her wings of gold in the

Navy and traversed the world, through discrimination and obstacles that would have grounded many others. Overcoming adversity became part of her daily life, from defiant ramp agents to sexist comments. Yet her boundary was clear—she was not just a woman; she was a qualified pilot, capable and determined to rise above.

Through all this, Pam leaned on the support of her tribe. Her daughter Catie was part of 18 different families by the time she was 16-years-old while Pam was away flying. It was a collective effort of love and care, a community raising Catie in the small town of Nokesville, VA.

These families became Pam's tribe, ensuring that while she broke glass ceilings in the air, her daughter was supported on the ground.

Pam's story is a testament to the power of questions, the grounding of rituals, the firmness of boundaries, and the strength of tribe. It's a reminder that with these Compass Points in place, we can soar—no matter the challenges.

Jill Marek's mother, Sharlea Leatherwood, was a trailblazer in every sense. She didn't let barriers hold her back. Instead, she embraced the power of inquiry to thread the needle of the path, always asking herself the critical question: "How can I move forward?" No matter the obstacles, she always found a way through.

After self-funding both her undergraduate degree and pharmacy school—while raising two young daughters—Sharlea became a pioneer in her field. She asked the right questions to clear her path, and in doing so, she started her own pharmacy business, growing it into three successful entities.

Sharlea's grounding ritual was simple but unwavering: "Pay it Forward." This steadfastness led her to become the first woman president of her state pharmacy association, then the state pharmacy board, and finally, the president of the National Community Pharmacy Association. Her commitment to her craft and ritual of service helped her break glass ceilings, navigate the challenges of large chains, leaving a legacy so strong that every year, the industry honors her with the "Trailblazer Award" in her name.

Boundaries were also a critical part of Sharlea's journey. Despite the obstacles and discrimination she faced as a woman in a male-dominated industry, she never allowed others to define her limitations. She set clear boundaries around her time, energy, and values, staying focused on her purpose. At home, she instilled in her daughters the importance of setting personal boundaries. She didn't simply guide them—she trusted them. Her oft-repeated phrase, "I trust you to make the right decision," became a cornerstone of her daughters' confidence. This unconditional belief in their judgment allowed them to grow into independent women, unafraid to follow their dreams.

Sharlea also knew the importance of Tribe. Although her work took her far and wide, she made sure her daughters were surrounded by a supportive community. Jill's Tribe was her mother and sister. Through Sharlea's unwavering trust and love, Jill was empowered to take risks and live boldly. Even after Sharlea's passing, her support continued in spirit, with her last message to Jill: "Follow your dreams."

In Jill's words: "Follow your dreams. That's what she always told me. And I believed her. Every part of my life that I value, every single thing I've done that is good and right, links back to her belief in me. She gave me the greatest gift—unconditional love and unwavering support. It gave me the courage to explore, to put myself out there. It's a rare thing, and I cherish it."

My mom, Catie's mom and Jill's mom are all badass and beautiful, and I'll bet you've had a role-model in your life who was too. The Compass is all about taking you where you want to go. If you look at the commonalities of these stories it is about "Keep Moving Forward." The Compass will take you in the direction you want to go.

Think of how they applied the Method of the Compass Rose to their lives. How did the power of Inquiry keep them *Stay True* on their paths? How did they make their way with grounding Rituals? What were the Boundaries necessary for success? Who was in their Tribe?

This is the gift of legacy. The deep value of what we have to offer each other. In this way, your decision to simply read and apply the concepts in this book is much larger than *you*.

By *living* this example and *staying true*, you inspire others to do the same... That's pretty epic and of huge importance. You have the power to break the *badass and beautiful* free within those around you—*Pass the Torch*!

To be badass is to have the courage to step into your truth and to be a force of nature—to unleash the wild woman at your core, whatever that means and looks like for you. To be beautiful is not to be quiet, timid or understated—it is to shine with raw truth, and truth is beautiful. Truth moves with grace and emotional intelligence. It doesn't *need* to force or push; it just *is*. For those who don't understand, they may admire from a distance, as if pondering the existence of a beautiful waterfall, awe-struck by the mystery of your magnitude. This is the power that I want to inspire in *my* daughter. This is the role model that I want to be *for her*.

Back when I was going through my divorce, when everything felt like a wild ride, the only thing I felt that I could control was what I did for my kids. And in retrospect that was all that *really* mattered.

Who looks up to you as a role model? Who do you *want* to be role model for? Who *could* you be a role model for? Ask yourself: "Am I being a *warning*, or am I being an *example*?"

One little spark of truth, your little spark, has the potential to ignite the masses. In fact, if you are living your truth, you are walking around lighting sparks, even if you don't realize it. People want *truth*. We are all craving it, especially in the chaos of today's world. We want someone who has lived through the lessons, who is willing to share, and who is honest with both themselves and others.

The Four Seasons hotel in Las Vegas has these enormous doors, and every time I walk in, I push them open with full force. In my mind, I am saying, "I have *arrived*." Every time someone comes to town, I take them to "the doors" to feel the sensation for themselves.

Then, *boom*, I walk in like a queen, with presence. It isn't about ego; it's about owning my worth... and knowing that I deserve to be there.

I offer this sense of worth back to you. You playing small—to fit in, to make other people feel more comfortable, to make other people feel bigger, to stay safe—doesn't serve the world. I invite you to walk through the doors of your life with force, with presence, with power, with ownership. I invite you to *arrive*.

As I think back to that Wild Woman poster that inspired me so many years ago, I wonder what your Badass and Beautiful woman looks like. I wonder how she moves? What she stands for? Who does she surrounds herself with? What's her story?

Do you wonder what your poster will look like? Use the QR Code to Generate a Poster to take all you have learned. Create a poster for to hang to inspire and feed your *Stay True* Flame.

All of that is up to you.

Welcome to the other side.

Welcome to your *Badass and Beautiful* Life.

12
CELEBRATE!

When we move through major milestones in life, it's easy to forget to pause and celebrate. However, the celebration is important part of integrating new growth. And the integration is what makes it *real*.

In Jewish traditions, we call this Bar (or Bat) Mitzvah—a celebratory graduation. Similar celebrations around the world include Quinceanera in Latin America, the Sunrise Ceremony in Apache traditions, Khatam Al Koran in Malaysia, Maasai in Tanzania, Ji Li or Guan Li in China, and Hamar Cow Jumping in Ethiopia.

I want you to know that I *see* you, all of you. Here you are graduating from these pages, ready to walk through the doors of your life with total *Badass and Beautiful* presence. Know that you revisit this book whenever you need it. Through these pages, I am always here for you and have your back.

As a sister in this badass and beautiful journey, *I believe in you in*, and I hope that we are able to meet in person someday. Come to one of my events. I'd love to see you there. *Own Your Worth* is every Spring on International Women's Day Weekend. The TRUE VOICE: *Intensive* is three times a year. If you truly want to connect, join my TLC Mastermind. You could also catch us at one of my Collective Luncheons near you or a Manifest Your _____ virtual Masterclass. If you feel moved to produce your own event, write your own content, or in any way create... visit Stay True Creative Productions Agency. Perhaps we can collaborate?

ALWAYS REMEMBER: *STAY TRUE* TO WHO YOU ARE.

ABOUT THE AUTHOR

LOREN LAHAV

Loren is an international thought leader, producer, mom, wife, author, entrepreneur, and philanthropist with more than 30 years of experience working alongside an extraordinary and dynamic array of world leaders, thought pioneers, and passionate truth seekers.

Loren has spoken to live audiences of tens of thousands and recently captivated a group of 160,000 on Zoom. Her career highlights include three decades of training leaders and consulting corporations of all sizes world-wide, including Fortune 500-companies in leadership, sales, communication, team-building, and company culture.

Loren has shared the stage with notable and celebrated luminaries such as Barbara Walters, Tony Robbins, Gary Vaynerchuk, Bob Proctor, Wayne Dyer, Carolyn Myss, Mike Rowe, Kevin O'Leary, Barbara Corcoran, Erin Brockovich, Campbell Brown, Robert Herjavec, Bear Grylls, Eric Worre and Jean Chatsky.

Hired by the Tony Robbins Company, now Robbins Research International (RRI), in 1990, she was instrumental in many of Tony's groundbreaking, transformational programs, serving audiences of up to 20,000 people. She facilitated over 300 of Tony Robbins' Companies Flagship immersive 5-day "Life Mastery Programs" onsite in Fiji. In Life Mastery, she has served over 10,000 people over the last 25-years. For two-decades, Loren created and oversaw Tony Robbins' Companies popular Crew Program. Most recently, collaborating to facilitate for Wealth Mastery Virtual to over 6,000 internationally as well as Life Mastery Virtual to over 10,000 internationally.

Driven by her passion to empower women from all walks of life, Loren has helped thousands of women around the globe rediscover, recognize, and own their unique value. She coaches women through stand-alone courses, events, retreats, and online programs. Over the last two-decades virtual and live events have included: *Lobella*, *Own Your Own Worth*, *Badass and Beautiful*, *Unapologetically Authentic*, *Manifest Your Magnificence* and *True Health Cleanse* all programs are geared at taking people through the processes of transformation in multiple areas of their lives. Loren's Podcast "*Stay True: Learn It, Love It, Live It!*" can be found on Apple.

MORE BOOKS
BY LOREN LAHAV

Loren is the author of five books and the creator of numerous life-changing products that have been distributed world-wide, such as her "I Am" cards for women, men, and kids. Loren's book titles include: "No Greater Love," "Chicken Soup for the Soul: Time to Thrive," "Drama Free Divorce Detox," "The Courage to Raise a Gentleman," "16-Week Reset Program," and "I AM Planner, 2023."

In addition to "Stay True: Own Your Badass and Beautiful Life," Loren Lahav's works include "No Greater Love," "Chicken Soup for the Soul: Time to Thrive," "Drama Free Divorce Detox," "The Courage to Raise a Gentleman," and the "16-Week Reset Program." The "I AM Planner 2025" is releasing now. In addition to her written work, Loren is the creator of life-changing products and events including her "I Am" cards for women, men, and kids, and the "Badass and Beautiful Cards." She is the Creator of Own Your Worth Experience, True Legacy Collective, and Co-Creator of the True Voice Intensive. Monthly, she collaborates with MyVegas, MyNashville, and MyAustin to host "OWN YOUR _____ Ladies' Luncheons" across the US. Loren also conducts an online global membership Own Your Manifestation where her Manifest Your Magnificence course and coaching program is run.

Stay True

OWN YOUR BADASS AND BEAUTIFUL LIFE

In addition to "Stay True: Own Your Badass and Beautiful Life," Loren Lahav's works include "No Greater Love," "Chicken Soup for the Soul: Time to Thrive," "Drama Free Divorce Detox," "The Courage to Raise a Gentleman," and the "16-Week Reset Program." The "I AM Planner 2025" is releasing now. In addition to her written work, Loren is the creator of life-changing products and events including her "I Am" cards for women, men, and kids, and the "Badass and Beautiful Cards." She is the Creator of Own Your Worth Experience, True Legacy Collective, and Co-Creator of the True Voice Intensive. Monthly, she collaborates with MyVegas, MyNashville, and MyAustin to host "OWN YOUR _____ Ladies' Luncheons" across the US. Loren also conducts an online global membership Own Your Manifestation where her Manifest Your Magnificence course and coaching program is run.

Stay True

OWN YOUR BADASS AND BEAUTIFUL LIFE

In addition to Stay True: Own Your Badass and Beautiful Life, Loren Lahav's works include No Greater Love, Chicken Soup for the Soul: Time to Thrive, Drama Free Divorce Detox, The Courage to Raise a Gentleman, and the 16-Week Reset Program. The I AM Planner 2025 is releasing now. In addition to her written work, Loren is the creator of life-changing products and events including her "I Am" cards for women, men, and kids, and the Badass and Beautiful Cards. She is the Creator of Own Your Worth Experience, True Legacy Collective, and Co-Creator of the True Voice Intensive. Monthly, she collaborates with MyVegas, MyNashville, and MyAustin to host "OWN YOUR _____" Ladies' Luncheons across the US. Loren also runs her online global membership Own Your Manifestation where her Manifest Your Magnificence course and coaching program is run.

LOREN LAHAV

Stay True

OWN YOUR BADASS AND BEAUTIFUL LIFE

In addition to Stay True: Own Your Badass and Beautiful Life, Loren Lahav's works include No Greater Love, Chicken Soup for the Soul: Time to Thrive, Drama Free Divorce Detox, The Courage to Raise a Gentleman, and the 16-Week Reset Program. The I AM Planner 2025 is releasing now.

In addition to her written work, Loren is the creator of life-changing products and events including her "I Am" cards for women, men, and kids, and the Badass and Beautiful Cards. She is the Creator of Own Your Worth Experience, True Legacy Collective, and Own Your Manifestation, as well as the Co-Creator of Own Your Magnificence and True Voice Intensive. Monthly, she collaborates with MyVegas, MyNashville, and MyAustin to host Ladies' Luncheons across the US.

Printed in the USA
CPSIA information can be obtained
at www.ICGtesting.com
CBHW020749301124
18177CB00038B/291